Out Of My Head

LEARNING TO REACH PEOPLE THROUGH THE ARTS

BILLY ARONSON

OUT OF MY HEAD
Learning to Reach People Through the Arts
By Billy Aronson

Published in the USA by:
BearManor Media
1317 Edgewater Dr #110
Orlando, FL 32804
www.bearmanormedia.com

Perfect ISBN: 979-8-88771-671-8
Case ISBN:979-8-88771-672-5
BearManor Media, Orlando, Florida

Printed in the United States of America
Book design by Robbie Adkins, www.adkinsconsult.com
Cover photo: Cristina Tarantola
Back cover photo: Lisa Vogel.

For Lisa Vogel

CONTENTS

CHAPTER 1.
BECOMING AN ARTIST

When I was 17 my first sexual relationship ended abruptly leaving me full of feelings and half-formed questions I couldn't begin to express. It all had to do with the way human beings try to reach each other, we use our eyes and our hands, press our whole bodies together and say things about love to get from inside these lonely selves we're stuck in to make some kind of meaningful contact, and though it's impossible to become one with another person we can still inch close enough to affect and comfort each other and make our lives feel beautiful. I had so much to say but when I tried to explain what was on my mind I could feel my back sweat as my words fell so far short.

It wasn't the first time I felt stuck inside my head.

In kindergarten my shyness earned me an S minus in Plays Well with Others. I wanted to share this sense I was getting of the coolness of the world but had no idea how until: at 8, while playing around on a toy organ I happened to press the first, third, and fifth keys at the same time. I played that major chord over and over until my middle finger accidentally hit the fourth key then went back to the third. I froze. My eyes teared up. That simple chord progression blew my little mind. I started playing every instrument I could get my hands on, at recess when the other boys were playing football I sang a song I'd made up ("One Girl" is the title and most of the lyrics) harmonizing with a friend while holding a Good & Plenty box like it was a microphone. At 14 I took my music onto the big stage with the middle school jazz ensemble; as I improvised a flute solo the metal tube was a conduit through which all my nervous excitement could flow from my head to the entire school. The girls said I was sensitive which in the 70s was a good thing, so I started acting and gave the school a sensitive Charlie Brown and a sensitive Romeo. Then senior year my love thing happened. I had something to scream about, but when I tried to let it out through the flute that didn't do it, I couldn't express this specific big thing with my music or through plays made by somebody else.

One Saturday night in the fall of my freshman year at Princeton I went to the library with a notebook and wrote out the goodbye conversation I had with my first girlfriend exactly as I remembered it. Then I outlined a series of scenes in which abstract characters inspired by my whole life would surround that dialogue so that when it was all performed on a stage other people could feel the enormous unexpressible whatever that was inside me. I walked back across campus feeling connected to everyone I knew and everyone I didn't know and to the stars overhead. I was a playwright.

You don't become an artist by completing a certain amount of work, reaching a particular level of achievement, or winning an honor or prize or praise from an expert. You become an artist by finding a creative way to express what's inside you and accepting that as your life. It's less a choice than a need. There's a glorious mess in your head and you don't want to be alone with it, you can't just tell people about it, it's too completely-your-own to be put into completely-not-your-own language, you need some creative way to get it out to the world and you feel this need very badly, it won't go away, so you devote yourself to grappling with sound, color, movement, words, reinventing old forms or inventing new ones, doing whatever you have to, to get that stuff out of your head to the world. In the old days they called it your fate. Now they say it's your DNA. I think of being an artist as a way I need to participate in life, to play well with others.

"You're so lucky to have found your path," my friends said. But what path? I couldn't see any path. A lot of the time I had no idea how to make my way from one step to the next, just the certainty that I had to keep going. Driven by impulses, hunches, and luck I went way out of my comfort zone, stumbling and falling down in a spectacular variety of ways. But with every failure I learned something. Eventually I figured out how to make my feelings accessible to an audience through my art, to use my talent to make money, to win accolades from my peers, to keep my work changing and my brain working over the course of a long career, and was even able to find true love and raise a family along the way. This book features the lessons that allowed me to do that. Though as a playwright/script writer/book writer/lyricist I've always been the word guy, I hope people pursuing any of the arts will find the lessons from my long strange trip helpful as they use their own idiosyncratic minds to create their work and establish a career.

I read in a book about writing that "unless you're Samuel Beckett" you should follow X, Y, and Z Basic Necessary Rules. In other words, unless you're some rare genius, do it the way everybody else has since the dawn of recorded time. As I see it, every artist is a rare genius. Each of us has a brain that's like nobody else's, so we need to find our own path to self-expression. Considered the greatest rock guitarist ever, Jimi Hendrix used his fists and his elbows and his teeth on the strings, he'd play it behind his back and wave it around turning the guitar into a phallus, a circus, a weapon that he'd use to blast the fire inside him out to the world. Though there's a place for tradition in the arts, in the end your work will be noticed not for the rules you follow but for the rules you break. My aim is to prod and provoke you to find your own rules, and to cheer you on.

I hope the book makes you feel great about what you're doing and proud to be an artist. For all the falling down my career has involved, I've totally loved it. It can go from terrifying to giddy crazy fun to crushing disappointment within the course of an hour, but through all the ups and downs it has always felt right for me. The life of an artist can be lonely; you're figuring out a path only you can see, working on problems that only you can solve. But artists everywhere are doing that every day. In your lonely struggle to get the indescribable stuff inside your head out to the world, you're not alone.

CHAPTER 2.
LEARNING TO FAIL

You arrive to an empty room, put up your posters and photos, fill the closets, drawers, and shelves. Before you know it you've got midterms, then fall break, finals, winter break, midterms, spring break, then you take down the posters and empty out the room for the summer. Within that rigid structure you're free to read all day, write papers all night, play any imaginable sport, play guitar in the courtyard, dance in the hall, run naked across campus, celebrate the team's victory with two thousand people, and pursue social connections that might one day help you get a job. College life is a vigorous swirl of activity that inside-his-own-head me always felt outside of. Luckily I found outsider friends with whom to carry out our own frenzied rituals in theaters across campus. We were actors, a few directors, and a playwright who hadn't written a play.

When I began playwriting in the fall of my freshman year I didn't know how to tell a story, create a character, establish a setting, or write useful stage directions. But I did have two things going for me: inspiration and ignorance. My inspiration was my first love affair; I was obsessed with finding a way to scream about that experience. And my ignorance was boundless. I had no idea how little I knew, which made writing a joyous adventure.

Every Saturday night I went to the library, set my notebook down at a desk, paced around while visualizing intensely and mumbling to myself, then dashed back to the notebook for a fit of passionate writing. Towards the end of freshman year I typed up a script of 60 pages (on erasable bond) that I felt was as profound as Einstein's theory of relativity and as mind-blowing as a Beatles concert.

The play I wrote, *Sea Fantasy*, was a wet dream about sex and the psychic forces it unleashes, with penis and vagina shaped objects strewn across the stage and eruptions of water and blood at climactic moments. When the campus theater wiz agreed to direct the play I skipped back to my dorm like a gleeful maniac. I submitted the script to Princeton's student-run Theater Intime, volunteered to work in the box office, befriended board members, ran lights for a show...anything that might sway them to do my theatrical wet dream. Though *Sea Fantasy* wasn't chosen for Intime's upcoming season the board did offer a workshop production. We'd have almost no budget for costumes, props, or sets, but so what? Actors would memorize the lines that I wrote and say them out loud, in front of live humans.

When the cast assembled for the first read-through I didn't need anyone to tell me which parts to cut, I had my sweat glands. By the end of the first page-long monologue my back was soaked. In those awful seconds I learned two huge differences between a novel and a play:

LESSON: A play is more like a fight than a work of literature.
If people tell stories in a play, they should be using their words like weapons to have a specific affect on somebody onstage and/or the audience.

LESSON: A play can't be boring. *Ever.*
If your mind wanders while you're reading a novel you can go back and figure out what's going on, or put it aside, get some fresh air, come back tomorrow. But with a play you're stuck in your seat. The play has to leap forward, surprise you constantly,

keep you engaged every moment or it becomes unbearable torture. That first draft of *Sea Fantasy* had lists of names, paragraphs of esoteric puns, and rambling monologues that had little to do with the rest of the play. I couldn't cut them fast enough.

Having a director was the best thing in the world; he could explain my script to the actors simply and clearly and stage the scenes in inventive ways that made them surprising even to me. As the actors got into their roles they became my heroes, each taking a specific humanoid hunch from my brain and giving it a tone of voice, a posture.

On opening night my Mom drove up from Philadelphia with my sister Dorothy and brother Joe who were still in high school. A few old friends from high school came, a few college friends...I stopped noticing things. As the house lights came down I took a seat in the front row and crossed my left ankle over my right knee. The stage lights came up. The play began. The house was silent. No sound. Everything felt stiff and awful. The actors were uncomfortable. The audience was sad. Nothing was making sense. A bunch of people had come together on a winter night to sit in a dark room for no reason. It was bad. It was bad. It was bad. It was bad. A few minutes into the play a character came downstage with a burst of energy and a couple members of the audience chuckled softly. The actors relaxed. The audience relaxed. I resumed breathing. The actors kept doing things. Saying things. With energy and personality and ease. When the house lights came up at the end of the play I realized one of my thighs was throbbing; I'd been frozen in position for an hour and twenty minutes. Afterwards my friends said nice things and I felt terrific.

For our second and final performance the next night Mom drove up by herself to see the play again. At the time I was at war with my mother. Her every attempt to get to know me felt like an invasion; I'd shut down, she'd cry, I'd close my door, she'd bang on the door and yell. So having her in the theater observing my private feelings felt wrong and embarrassing but it was also great; as she sat quietly in back of the theater it was like I was a little kid sitting beside her on the couch again and I could open up to her about everything that was on my mind.

LESSON: Through art you can expose yourself from a distance.

The next day I heard that the *Princeton Shopping News* had reviewed our show so I took a bus to the mall, grabbed a paper from the pile outside the McDonald's and flipped through the pages until I found the words in bold face: "*Sea Fantasy* is a Bomb". Bombs are explosive, right? So that's good?

It was not good. The critic described her experience of sleeping through this pretentious display of college students having a fling with theater. She hated every word of my play. In that instant a feeling rushed through my entire body for the first time, though not the last, this terrible sense that the things inside my head are weird and bad and wrong so I will always be alone. But by the time the bus arrived back on campus I had convinced myself that the woman who wrote the review and her intended readers weren't nearly cool enough to be in my audience anyway and the reviewer herself was an idiot.

Over time though I came to realize that most of my classmates who'd seen the play didn't understand it either; they couldn't tell where the characters were or what was going on, they got that it was about teen romance but didn't feel nearly the power or sense of importance I wanted to convey. So those quiet audiences weren't astounded, on the verge of tears...they were quietly confused and/or bored.

Out of the whole play there was a section of maybe one minute that actually got a response, during a scene in which an old man character is talking to a female manikin. As he tells the manikin about his high school days he describes the love scene in his school play as being so passionate that everyone in the audience started touching themselves in sensual ways. One reason our audience laughed and gasped is because of the explicit content (this was 1977). But *Sea Fantasy* had other sexual stuff that didn't cause a stir. This particular passage engaged the audience because it was about them. As the character talked about another audience touching themselves, the play was winking at this audience, teasing them, reaching into their laps.

From this sliver of theater I learned so many things:

LESSON: Art should be about what people are dealing with now.

A play can tell the story of a childhood in Queens in the 60s or a planet populated by ducks in the next millennium as long as it's ultimately about what people in the audience are concerned with at this moment.

LESSON: What's most important is not what the characters are doing to each other, but what the show is doing to the audience.

Drama teachers will tell you that a play is characters in conflict; the more tension between the characters the more powerful the play. But the fact is, a play about two tramps waiting for something to happen can rock your world too.

LESSON: Create stuff that really turns you on.

That *Sea Fantasy* monologue to the manikin was a breathless thrill to write, so I learned the importance of being driven by a kind of reckless lust while writing. In other words: Don't write scenes that give you the fine pleasure of getting your room all in order or fixing yourself a lovely breakfast, unless you're writing them to set up scenes that give you the outrageous chills of jamming with John Coltrane or getting naked with the yoga teacher of your dreams.

LESSON: To grab an audience you have to go to extremes.

There are no limits to how great a work of art can be. If you're headed in the right direction, go go go go. But the main lesson I learned from my first play was:

LESSON: Art needs focus.

A play can go all over the place as long as everything's connected in a specific way to one central story or theme or something. In my eagerness to get everything from my 18 years on earth into *Sea Fantasy* I confused pretty much everybody. Though I learned a ton from the experience, in terms of getting my feeling about the wondrous-whatever-that-passes-between-two-people from my head to the audience, it failed.

LESSON: The first time you fail you're sure you'll get it right next time.

For my next play, I chose a simpler, more direct story with only two characters so the audience could focus on the contact between them. *A Twilight* was about two mimes in black leotards and tights who are doing their silent routine miming objects when they suddenly find actual objects on the stage and words coming out of their white-faced heads. The strangeness of speaking had become an obsession of mine sophomore year. On a first date (that did not lead to a second) I was told, "You need to stop noticing the way I'm saying things and pay attention to what I'm saying." But I couldn't. The sounds, rhythms, and gestures people use to communicate were far more interesting to me than what they were trying to say. I suppose that's one reason I'm drawn to the theater; unlike in the more literal mediums of film and TV, on a stage the simple fact that someone is standing there breathing, gesturing, and talking can be made to seem odd and worth examining.

When *A Twilight* was performed in a small black box theater some viewers found it to be a Rorschach test: A friend thought it was about her relationship with her boyfriend and that I'd been eavesdropping on them, a student who was leading protests against Apartheid said the play showed how language can be used to keep people down, my mother thought it was about my relationship with her and that the end showed a hint of forgiveness. Though I hadn't consciously written about any of those things, each viewer had picked up on something that was bouncing around in my head.

LESSON: As you express yourself through the arts, things come out of your head that you didn't know were in there.

As with my last play, there was a particular moment audiences responded to in *A Twilight*, a nasty fight near the end. After the mimes learn to use words to form a personal connection, the female mime uses words to trap and attack the male mime. Eventually he goes into a rage, knocking down all the objects they've arranged and hurling them in all directions. As sharp words and blunt objects flew, audience members sat up, mouths fell open.

LESSON: Bodies in motion is good.

LESSON: Objects in motion is good.

LESSON: War is good.

But the main thing I learned from *A Twilight* was:

LESSON: Even with a single, focused story, the audience can have no idea what's going on.

My play about how hard it is to speak to another person failed to speak to most other persons. My peers said they didn't understand it, or as we had learned to say more pretentiously by junior year, they found it "inaccessible". They weren't sure who the characters were or what was going on. So once again I'd failed to reach the audience.

LESSON: The second time you fail you're sure you'll get it right next time.

For my next and final college play there was no way people weren't going to understand what was going on, so I borrowed a story that was already famous.

LESSON: When you can't think of a good story, steal a great one.

I based my third play on Vergil's *Aeneid*. The story of its central lovers Dido and Aeneas has been told and loved and understood for thousands of years. The other characters are Roman gods and classical heroes that everyone already knows. Intime granted me a full production as part of their season, which meant we'd have an audience of students from all over campus and subscribers from town. Hundreds of people I didn't even know would see this one.

The director, a local professional director named Carol MacVey, had a gift for making people feel appreciated, so even the most insecure college actors could let down their guards and be vulnerable in a group. At one rehearsal, to help the cast relate to the theme of letting go, Carol set up a group exercise in which our Dido and Aeneas were told to hold onto each other as the rest of the cast tried to separate them. As the others lifted our Dido actress away she clung to Aeneas as hard as should could, then she lost it completely, kicking and grabbing, clinging to his shoulders then his shirt, sobbing loudly out of control, everything inside this poor young woman was spilling out. (The actress's parents were getting divorced at the time and her boyfriend was always yelling at her; maybe these things had something to do with the outburst.) Soon everyone in the room was in tears, including Carol and me. Afterwards we had a big group hug and went to a party, and as we were jumping around to disco music it struck me that if we could get that much wild emotion out of Dido and Aeneas, the audience would feel the power of human contact between lovers that I felt with my first lover and that thing inside my head would finally be out there. I jumped higher and higher on the dance floor.

On opening night Carol got me to sit next to her, which took some convincing; I'd taken in my last play mostly from backstage in fetal position, occasionally venturing out to stand in back of the house jerking around as though being electrocuted. As I watched *Aeneas* from the fourth row I spent a lot of time yanking my curly locks out to their fullest extension...until people started responding to the play's light-hearted subplot by emitting the vocable HA. Although I'd intended that part of the play to be funny, I never considered what it would be like if a bunch of people laughed out loud, consistently. My plays were supposed to be serious and sensitive like me, designed to give the audience that grand feeling of being chilled and moved. And yet people kept going HA.

LESSON: As people begin to get you, you might be surprised what they get.

After the first weekend's performances newspapers all over New Jersey panned my script. As I tried to read the reviews my eyes kept bouncing off the page, though I did notice the word "sophomoric" appearing a lot. Again I had that awful feeling that the world will never get me. I puzzled over the reviews, heard from students and teachers, and learned a few more painful lessons:

LESSON: Broad comedy can be like babies, animals, or nudity on stage - when it's there you don't notice anything else.

The wacko subplot with its sexual puns and gigantic phallus made of Silly Putty overshadowed the sober main story of our hero, so the play didn't work overall.

LESSON: Sentiment is the enemy of true feeling.

When writing the reunion scene in the underworld between Dido and Aeneas, I needed the audience to feel Aeneas' love for Dido so I had him shout I love you eight times. Emotion has to be earned through specific action that expresses the character's unique heart, not by having the character tell us what he's feeling, loudly, eight times. The actors never reached the level of genuine emotion we'd found in the separation exercise, and my script never earned it.

LESSON: It's not enough for an audience to understand what's happening on stage if they don't understand why they should care.

Everybody knew Aeneas was trying to make it from the flames of Troy to a new home in Italy. But because I hadn't written him as a character they could relate to, they didn't get why they should care. So a lot of people came out saying, "I'm not sure what it was really about," or "What point were you making?" or, again:

"I didn't understand your play." Why was it so hard for me to be understood?

LESSON: When your work fails to do what you want it to, audiences can still find things to enjoy.

Though the reviews kept the grownups from town away, the theater continued to fill with students who seemed to enjoy my sophomoric romp.

For the last performance my Dad flew in from Oklahoma to see a play of mine for the first time. Dad was a brilliant, compassionate man but he had trouble asking the sort of specific questions about my life that would make me feel he cared. When I'd visit him with his new family I struggled to impress my Dad and always left feeling that I'd failed. But on that last night of *Aeneas* the cast turned in their best performance and I could see Dad smiling the whole time, at one point he even went HA. Afterwards my Dad put his *Aeneas in Flames* ticket with my name on it in his wallet where he kept it for the rest of his life.

LESSON: Your art gives others a chance to expose themselves to you.

Another thing happened after that last performance that I'd never forget: A guy leaving the theater said "That was a good play" as he put his around arm a woman's shoulder; she nodded and leaned into him as they walked away.

LESSON: Through art you can be part of the lives of people you don't even know.

When I came home for spring break Mom wanted to talk. My mother talks all the time, but when she "wants to talk" that can only be bad. After cornering me in her bedroom and shutting the door:

MOM: So what are your plans for after you graduate?
BILLY: I'm going to move to New York to make it as a playwright.
MOM: (deadly silence)
BILLY: I'll make money during the day and at night I'll write my
    plays.

MOM: Plays people can understand? (she'd read the reviews)
BILLY: Yes plays people can understand.
MOM: And how are you going to make money?
BILLY: Washing pots.
MOM: Do you realize how expensive it is to live in New York?
BILLY: I'll live in a tiny apartment and eat cereal and slices of
    pizza.
(Mom is crushed, stunned, miserable, verge of tears. After more
    deadly silence:)
MOM: Billy. Promise me you won't wind up living in a garret.
BILLY: (making a quick exit) I won't wind up living in a garret.

Luckily I didn't know what a garret was or that in New York you're
lucky to find an affordable garret.

Back at school, on a sunny Saturday morning a letter
swooped through the mail slot in my door and sailed halfway
across the room. It was from the only grad school I'd applied to,
Yale Drama School. Accepted to the playwriting program! With
enough financial aid/work/loan to make it affordable. I'd be writing my plays at the most famous drama school in the country.

At the end of the school year the weather gets hot, everybody goes in different directions, and I'm there holding tight to
memories so I don't slide into a funk. But as the end of college
approached I started having euphoric flying dreams.

**LESSON: The third time you fail you realize that expressing
your most intimate self through the arts is extremely hard but
you feel proud just to be taking baby steps in that direction.**

I'd come to see the theater as a laboratory where you can
combine big emotions with big ideas. It was a serious, sacred
place, but with all the dance and sexual energy and laughter it
was a party too, and a jam session where you make music out of
human life. I also saw theater as the ultimate form of romance in
which you share your love with everyone you know and everyone
you don't know. None of what I'd written so far would work off
campus, I knew that, and I had no idea how I'd ever get the world

outside my head to understand the world inside it. But what if the all-star professors at Yale could teach me how to write real plays for the real world...plays that people would understand?

※ ※ ※

CHAPTER 3.
LEARNING WHOM TO BELIEVE

The first play of mine presented at the Yale Drama School featured four gifted attractive actors. Scripts in hand, they moved among four folding chairs on a classroom floor for an audience of actors, directors, playwrights, dramaturgs and professors. As I sat among all those chosen people I had no place to hide and contort so I wrote in my notebook "Reality is the thing that is happening now and now it is happening the reality that is happening now is reality happening now now now it is happening now..." etc. looking up when people laughed at the play, then back to my scribbled babble.

After the presentation America's most influential theater critic Richard Gilman said he liked the opening stage direction that called for simply "Two beds" – it reminded him of the plays of Samuel Beckett – and said I should make the dialogue more spare. Famous playwright John Guare said he liked the main character's vulnerability but wished the play was more than just "one potato chip." Though nothing ever came of my short play, I responded to both Gilman's and Guare's suggestions, alternately trimming and expanding the script for years. I was determined to respond to every note given to me at the Yale Drama School.

To get all name dropping out of the way, over my 3 years at Yale: Frances McDormand had me over for macaroni and cheese, Kate Burton dropped by to visit my room mate and saw me in my underpants, I played the Fool to Charles "Roc" Dutton's *King Lear* in an acting class, I played piano for a cabaret show hosted by Tony Shaloub, David Allen Greer and Patricia Clarkson were in staged readings of plays of mine, I had a crush on an actress who was in love with John Turturro, and I got to call Angela Bassett "Angie".

Many of my Yale classmates would become famous but everybody was good. The actors were all vibrant and attractive. The directors all had bold ideas and charisma. There were designers, stage managers, aspiring producers, and critics...Theater undergrads from across the country had come together to form an all-star community, the theater of tomorrow. At the center of it all was the playwright. Everybody was looking for scripts to work on. No more begging my friends to audition; amazing actors would be assigned to work on our plays whether they liked it or not.

Of the 18 playwrights in the school, nearly all had taken time off after college to explore their art in the real world. When one of my classmates realized I'd come straight out of college she said no wonder I still seemed "wet behind the ears". She was right. I was an innocent, wide open, ready to listen to anyone who could show me the way to get my inspirations out from between my wet ears to the world.

Our guide through three years of playwriting was our avuncular chairman Oscar Brownstein. "Okkie", as he liked to be called, read every draft of every play we wrote and was constantly looking for ways we could improve. The focus of Okkie's teaching was the perception shift, a climactic moment built into a play when the audience suddenly sees things in a different way; maybe they go from rooting for a hero to succeed only to realize he never had a chance. I'd been writing plays from beginning to end, groping towards a climax. But Okkie had us outline our stories first so this orgasm of audience insight would be guaranteed.

After writing a script we wouldn't have to wait for a full production to find out if it was any good; we could hear it read aloud in class and get instant feedback from classmates and scholars. As Okkie said to the class before my first cold reading, "We're here to tell Billy what he can't know on his own." Okkie felt that as a playwright you can't see what's wrong with your play, you need other people to tell you. If you're at a restaurant and someone says there's egg on your face, you don't get defensive or make excuses, you say oh my god thank you and wipe off the egg. There was a whole development process in place as a play goes from reading to staged reading to workshop production, with feedback following each step, until you're learning what's on your face from Drama School Dean Lloyd Richards himself.

The first play I wrote at Yale was based on the short novel *Lenz*, George Buchner's story of a playwright who's losing his mind. In my first draft of the script I had Lenz interact with a bodiless "Voice" when he's alone in nature to dramatize his particular madness. When we presented this version to the class, the chairman of the directing program and guest professor George Roy (*Butch Cassidy and the Sundance Kid*) Hill agreed that the Voice character was confusing and weird and that the other characters didn't feel quite real, I should cut the Voice and fill out the other characters so they'd be easier to relate to. I thanked the wise men and the classmates who echoed their critique, and couldn't wait to make the changes. Though the play worked inside my head as I'd written it, with this clear unanimous direction from the people outside my head, I hoped to get everyone to feel the love I felt for Lenz.

When I brought the new draft into class the professors had more ideas for how to improve it. My classmates had ideas. Friends visiting classmates had ideas. The guy in the back visiting from the local bar had ideas. I wanted to please them all. Kept bringing it back. Kept getting suggestions. And as I did I came to realize:

LESSON: Presenting your work in class gets old.

People aren't there to see a show. They're there to visualize a show, which is more work than fun. If it goes well your peers are happy for you and jealous. If it goes poorly they're sad for you and relieved. Nobody actually sits back and enjoys your play. So you lose a sense of why you're doing what you've chosen to do with your entire life.

LESSON: Graduate school is not like college.

College is about the overall experience, you're there to explore, find yourself, socialize, there's a whole team of people making sure you're growing "as a person". In graduate school nobody cares about any of that. You're there to learn your subject and get out. There's no freshman counselor, dorm advisor, or sorority-sister to help when you start to wonder what the hell you're doing.

And we playwrights had so much time free to wonder what we were doing. Aside from 3 hours or so a week of class time, playwrights had all day free to write. I'd write a couple hours, notice it was 11 AM, too soon for lunch, then I'd think about writing, think about money, think about thinking, wander the streets of New Haven wondering why I was borrowing money to prepare for a career that doesn't pay, why hadn't I become a doctor like my Dad who was helping people every day and getting paid?

For fall break I got away from campus as fast as I could to visit friends. Those who were in grad school for writing/art/music/ acting were asking the same questions I was, as were friends approaching careers in the arts right out of college. What had we gotten ourselves into? How would we ever do those grownup things like buy TVs and have children?

I was most eager to visit the Haverford College freshman who was the closest person in the world to me at the time, my Matie-Mate, my little bro' Joe. While I was cerebral and brooding, Joe was my comic relief who could keep things real; he was a track star, drank beer, and had lots girlfriends, all of which I envied. Through years of sharing bunk beds and small rooms Joe and I had evolved our own language based on Monty Python, Looney Tunes, and countless inside jokes.

When I caught up with my brother in his dorm room we jumped around and hugged and called each other IDJUT (the way Yosemite Sam says "idiot"), but as we began to talk Joe seemed preoccupied. In mid-conversation he slid under his desk then sprung up and bumped his head. His stunt had the rhythm of a joke but I didn't get it. He apologized, said something about how hard things had been lately and started tearing pages out of his notebook—another joke? Then he politely asked me to leave. I took it personally, assumed he was having academic problems, maybe felt threatened by me in some way.

When I got back to campus I came down with a fever, stayed in bed shivering and sweating for pretty much the whole week. When the fever was gone I stayed in bed another day, then got out of bed and stood there crying. There was nothing to do, no reason to move. I went to a rehearsal for *Lenz*, we made small talk about fall break, the scenes were going well. But afterwards, that same emptiness. I didn't know what to say about it, there was nothing to say.

After a week of feeling crappy I called Mom to tell her I was depressed and she asked if I could transfer to the law school. (Every drama school parent's secret wish?) When I explained that Yale doesn't work like that Mom had some advice that was excellent for me and for artists everywhere who need to avoid sinking under the weight of their thinking:

LESSON: Exercise.

LESSON: Make plans with other people.

LESSON: Play music.

LESSON: Volunteer.

LESSON: Get busy and stay busy and no matter what: don't sit around thinking.

Mom's own bouts with depression had made her wise about the ways of recovery.

Right away I gave myself a strict routine that included:

1) Pushups and situps every morning to be done the instant I wake up — Must get through that toughest moment of the day quickly and not just lie there despairing.

2) Trip to the library — So important for an introspective artist to get out of the room. At the library I'd gather books from the shelves, browse through them, write questions and thoughts about plays/dreams/life in my notebook, read, write, pace, get the cinnamon crumb cake from the vending machine, whatever. Every day, all around the world, people were going into the office, sitting through tedious meetings, failing to make any tangible progress, and coming home feeling just fine because they'd "put in a day's work". My trip to the library gave me that sense of going somewhere. When I read and paced but didn't write I assured myself I was building potential energy that would someday become kinetic.

3) At the end of the day I'd go for a long run with my philosophy grad student friend Larry who lived across the hall. As we took our daily jog Larry could explain complex moral philosophical questions for nearly an hour as I huffed and puffed. The deep breathing felt good. So did seeing the hills and the sky, and thinking about anything but work. And at the end, nature's sweet anti-depressant: endorphins.

Taking Mom's suggestion to volunteer I signed up for weekly shifts pushing stretchers at St. Raphael's Hospital. What a relief to have somewhere to be, something to do. One of my first patients to transport was an elderly woman who lay still in the stretcher, eyes closed, so emaciated she seemed barely alive. When we stopped at an elevator she opened her mouth and twisted up her face as though howling, without making a sound. As I stared at the woman's anguished face the PA-in-training saw me tearing up and pulled me aside to explain that the best we can do for the patients is keep things pleasant, ask how their soap opera is going, stay upbeat; if I let myself feel as bad as the patient I won't do anyone any good. He was right. Upbeat small talk was good for the patients and for me.

My next volunteer gig was at a mental ward in a veteran's hospital where I created scenes for the patients to perform. The one that went best was a divorced father/estranged daughter scene I wrote for a male patient suffering from PTSD and a female patient who'd been sexually abused. They spoke their lines with caution, honest but tentative, releasing just a teeny bit of the rage and sadness they each had inside, staying in character, as they made it through to a moment of tender forgiveness. It was the first time I felt proud of what I'd written since college. **LESSON: Making art for those in need feels so good to the needy artist.**

Determined to spend less time in the room, one sunny afternoon I let my feet wander around campus like hands on a Ouija board and wound up at a children's theater where a group of undergrads was performing a joyful rhyming hodgepodge for an audience of kids. Unlike at the Drama School, the actors weren't doing this to satisfy a requirement, impress teachers, or further their careers, and audiences hadn't come out of any sense of obligation. Everybody was there to have a good time, period. Actors loved their lyrical lines. Kids laughed, sang, cheered characters on, or fell asleep. The play had no explicit message but reminded viewers of some basic truths we all need to remember: **LESSON: Music is fun. Language is fun. It's cool to be alive.** When I told the director how much I loved the show she invited me to write a play for their summer season. In response I wrote my first children's play, *Angry Ingrid,* about a girl who decides to turn the boring world upside down. Writing without an outline I let the characters go wherever their goofy rhyming language took them. If Ingrid's Cat wanted to eat the sun, no problem. When the play had gone on long enough I had the characters break into song and fly away. I loved writing that way and loved the result.

LESSON: Always improvise.

Ever since writing my first children's play I try to stay relaxed and open to the unexpected in every draft of my grownup plays, no matter how tight the structure. Though musicians playing a Beethoven symphony can't improvise by changing the notes, they can still listen to one another, sense the audience, respond to the feeling of the moment so every note is a discovery, as though they're playing the piece for the first time.

When *Angry Ingrid* was read in playwriting class, John Guare said it was better than my other plays because I was writing for an audience that I thought would love me. He was right. I feel comfortable with kids. So as I wrote for an audience of kids I felt uninhibited, free to take risks.

LESSON: Imagine an audience that loves you.

Meanwhile I was laboring over *Lenz*, making it cleaner and clearer draft after draft, until the play was finally performed... and the audience was hushed. Stunned silence? Awe? Dean Lloyd Richards shook my hand and said, "So you're the playwright!" (exclamation point mine) Overall people found *Lenz* dry, restrained, and hard to get into, even though I'd listened to everything everyone said and did exactly what they told me.

LESSON: You can do exactly what people tell you to do and still not please them.

My brother was getting feedback too at this time, from voices inside his head. In a letter he let me know that he was wearing two hats on campus, dancing by himself in public, grabbing food off people's plates. A couple weeks later he called me from the college infirmary to ask if I ever hear voices telling me to do crazy things. I told him he was talking about impulses, sure I have them, but you learn to ignore them. Joe was unable to do that. Before completing his second semester he followed voices in his head that told him to travel the country, sleep in trees, eat out of garbage bins, show up at the homes of friends of mine telling them he was me. He gave my father his track trophies, buried one of my old flutes somewhere in New Jersey, put the other in a mailbox in Cincinnati, all for reasons that made perfect sense to Joe. He picked up a baby from a stroller, was beaten up by the dad and arrested. Eventually my parents were able to work together to track Joe down, have him analyzed and diagnosed as schizophrenic.

Playwrights are constantly questioning. Why is the character doing this now? Is it believable? Why should anyone care? What am I doing? Why do I just keep doing what I'm doing? Why did this terrible thing happen to my brother and not me? In a world of pointless random suffering what difference does it make if anyone writes a play? Isn't there something else I should be doing? **LESSON: When you lose a sense of what you're doing, take a break from doing it.**

By the end of the academic year I'd had enough of waking up and wondering what to write and wanted to affect people in a more direct way. I took leave from Yale, applied to VISTA (the AmeriCorps of its day) for a job fighting poverty in America, and was placed in rural North Carolina to serve as a community educator.

If I'd wanted to get away from theater for some perspective, this was the place. The only theater in all of Chatham County was a drive-in outside of Siler City that showed XXX movies. Five days a week I'd put on a tie and jacket and pants that were not jeans and go into an office to write educational materials. On weekends I'd spread the word about social programs and benefits, driving on unnamed rural routes behind big trucks packed with chickens or small trucks with rifles hanging in the back window on my way to churches, community groups, and unheated shacks where children had black spotted teeth. At night I'd get stoned and stare at the stars and wonder how people who had so little could be so much more self-confident than I was. At every community meeting locals would proclaim: "I'm thankful just to be able to wake up in the morning." "I'm happy just to see the sun another day." They seemed to have no big questions, only answers that gave them strength. At church they'd clap and cheer as the reverend spoke with driving rhythm. Every so often an elderly woman would spring to her feet and start shouting Yes Jesus and dancing in the aisle in ecstasy as though possessed. At one church service a minister advised his flock to "Learn from the Jews. They'll steal the shirts off your backs but they're God's chosen people." Suddenly it struck me: I'm a Jew. All I could remember from a brief stint in Hebrew School when I was 7 were those triangular cookies with a prune in the middle, and a painting in the lobby of men with white beards arguing. I didn't tell anyone in the South I was Jewish but people seemed to sense it; they kept asking about my religion and I kept changing the subject. I definitely stuck out. Was there something Jewish about the way I talk? My face? My name? Who is this Jew that I am and what does he believe?

I found an answer to the last question when I went to Durham to see jazz trumpet player Donald Byrd. The opening act featured a skinny pianist with long messy hair who was wearing some kind of black bedroom slippers. As he slunk to the piano I couldn't imagine this frail shy guy anywhere but on the stage; he seemed way too delicate for the world. His playing was fine, timid, until suddenly he started jerking around, flailing his hands at the keyboard in a frenzy of atonal improvisation. He wasn't trying to play melodies or entertain anybody or even thinking about music; as desperate as a fish flopping in the dirt, he needed to strike those keys to breathe. After his set the pianist in black scurried off to polite applause and disappeared but my heart was still beating fast. I wanted to throw off my tie and jacket and mess up my hair and be that guy. Reasoning can never lead anyone to a life in the arts. It's not a reasonable thing to do. You have to feel it inside you and just believe.

LESSON: Being an artist requires faith.

Questioning, despairing, dreaming and failing are the artist's way of dancing in the aisle. I missed it so much. There are people who are meant to give their love to the world by working in a hospital or doing social work. That type of work comes naturally to them, they enjoy it, they're good at it, and I admire those people a lot. But I'm an artist. I give my love by creating.

When I returned to New Haven my faith in my art was strong but I was still searching for a god or gods to guide me. The teachers at the School seemed most excited by family plays with a kitchen sink so I tried to write a family play with a kitchen sink.

LESSON: It's great to stretch yourself, try something different, as long as you can snuggle into the different and make it your own.

Unfortunately I could never snuggle into kitchen sink naturalism. Way out of my comfort zone, I retreated into my left brain, land of the tidy and safe, instead of the right brain where the wild things are, so the realistic play I wrote was awful.

Finally in my last year I came up with something both unrealistic and intensely personal. *Swan Lake Moon* was about a young prince who falls in love with a swan as the world around him becomes unintelligible and splits apart. Unlike my *Lenz*, this play dealt with a madness that was vivid and painful for me. I was beginning to deal with my feelings about my brother's mental illness, with help from a therapist who told me:

LESSON: When something happens to someone you love, it happens to you.

At first I felt guilty about putting my brother's suffering into my work, but finally came to accept that I had no choice.

LESSON: Your loved one's pain is your pain too. So you can and must use it.

The director assigned to work with me on *Swan Lake Moon* was confused and grossed out by the sexual/fecal imagery so I pulled back on the weird nastiness and made the play more witty and clever. As we brought in actors the play became even more witty and clever and was deemed worthy of a staged reading for the heads of the directing, acting, dramaturgy, and playwriting programs. When we presented my play to these VIPs they found it silly, snide, and pointless and so did I. By untwisting the twistedness I'd destroyed whatever was good in my own script.

LESSON: If you do what people tell you, they might actually despise the result.

The complete disconnect between the cool scenes I saw in my head and the screeching stupidity they turned into when presented in front of people left me feeling helpless and utterly lost as my time at Drama School was coming to an end.

But luckily, while we were rehearsing for the staged reading, Okkie had made the genius decision to connect me with Lawrence Kornfeld, a visiting director who'd been part the most adventurous theater groups of the 60s and 70s. At Okkie's suggestion I had given Lawrence the second draft of my *Swan Lake* play that pleased my director, but I also gave him the first draft that the director found confusing and gross.

A couple weeks after that miserable reading Lawrence and I met at my favorite bagel place where he told me he found the first draft nasty, funny, full of problems but original, it left him anxious to see where I'd gone from there. But when he started the next draft he hated it so much he threw it across the floor. He found it empty, shallow, full of clichés, a huge step backwards.

YES. It felt so great to hear an official acknowledgment of what I'd been sensing all along: The whole play development system at the Yale Drama School was exactly wrong for me. The clear, sober, realistic plays about family that were championed at the School can be terrific. But the world of those plays feels nothing like the world I know. Daft distorted chaos is my home. With all the feedback I'd gotten on my plays, no one ever said, "We have no idea what you're trying to do so ignore every word of our feedback, run screaming from the classroom now because we're bound to attack the most interesting and original features, they're just sticking out there so unusual and easy to bombard, and if you do what we tell you your work will get worse and worse and you'll lose faith in yourself and become dependent on our guidance until your work is so bad you'll lose all sense of why you started writing in the first place." That feedback I could have used.

LESSON: The presumption that "the more people who give input the better the product" may work in politics or fast food but can be harmful in the arts.

Speaking generally about playwriting, Lawrence had suggestions I remember vividly 40 years later:

LESSON: To find an idea, let your mind go; Where does your mind go when you piss?

LESSON: Write about what you're going through now but disguise it.

LESSON: If you're going to be funny, be *really* funny.

LESSON: Write what pisses you off. Are you political? Maybe you're liberal, maybe you're conservative.

LESSON: Instead of taking a little breath before you start, take a deep breath. Instead of looking down the block, look all the way down the road.

LESSON: A story can take any shape, it doesn't have to go in a straight line. (He picked up a napkin, crumpled it, pulled it taut and held it up.) This shape isn't linear, but it's fascinating.

LESSON: Obscene language? What's obscene? Everybody says those words.

At this point I was so excited to write I could hardly sit still. After telling Lawrence I was going to take all his suggestions and write a play I was proud of, I asked if I could show him that next play when it's done. Lawrence's response to this question was the most startling and wonderful thing he told me: No.

LESSON: You don't need anyone else to tell you if your work is good. You know.

Lawrence Kornfeld was right. I'd never given anyone two different drafts of the same play to read. Who does that? It's rude. But at some level I knew the draft I wrote for myself was better than the revision that pleased others. By refusing to read my next play Lawrence caused a flip in my head -- a perception shift. Though the tell-me-if-I-have-egg-on-my-face-somebody-please approach to play development works in terms of simple, fixable adjustments, when it comes to significant decisions about what to write and how to write it, no one else can help you. In the end, you have to listen to your own intuitions, trust your own judgment, and believe most deeply in yourself.

At graduation many of my Yale Drama School classmates had agents, auditions, cool connections, or polished scripts to take to New York. I on the other hand was happy to have made it through the past 4 years with a working brain. Though I hadn't figured out how to tell a big story, how to use humor to express serious feelings, or how to make a play understandable without destroying it, I had learned to ignore voices that didn't serve me. So after listening to everything I'd been told, I resolved to put nearly all of it aside and figure things out on my own. And that, in the end, is how to write a play.

❋ ❋ ❋

CHAPTER 4:
LEARNING TO LOOK

As I drove the rented van containing all my worldly goods into Manhattan I needed to turn right but people kept walking in front of me. Even as I edged into the crosswalk, even when the light was against them, those New Yorkers just kept coming. Eventually I got it: The only way to get through was to make it clear to these people that if they didn't stop walking I would kill them. And that's why I love New York. It's an entire city of people as obsessed with getting somewhere as I am.

With no teachers to guide me or peers to impress I was free to figure out my craft on my own. Through college and grad school my writing had been driven by personal relationships and works of literature. In New York I discovered a new way to find inspiration:

LESSON: You can take your art to another level by observing the world around you.

Of course, before you can take your art anywhere in the "real world", you have to attend to certain basic necessities. I thought I'd support myself by teaching high school, but after writing to two-dozen schools and being granted three interviews I got zero offers. I searched the *New York Times* want ads and applied for anything remotely related to writing but nobody wanted me. I was resigned to using my dishwashing skills to support myself when a friend hooked me up with a job at the ferocious corporate law firm of Skadden, Arps, Slate, Meagher, and Flom. As a "night paralegal" my mission was to help lawyers race to prepare massive documents for global distribution through the night by proofreading, xeroxing, mailing, and assisting in various other ways; my specialty was sending out for Chinese food. Working until 2 AM three nights a week I earned enough to cover my rent and loan repayments as long as I didn't do anything crazy like buy a pair of shoes or see a dentist.

The clients at Skadden, Arps were big rich companies that were trying to get bigger and richer. Though some artists won't accept a money gig unless it makes the world better in some way, the way I see it: the world desperately needs to dance and laugh and scream and see what's goin' on in a fresh way. So:

LESSON: The most noble thing artists can do is make money as quickly as possible and get back to making the world dance/laugh/scream/see.

The sleep-deprived Skadden lawyers could be short-tempered and I got sick of pretending to care about their impenetrable documents, but I loved my peers on the night staff. Painters, writers, musicians, actors, dancers, creators of every kind, we formed a supportive community of artists struggling to make it in the City. Between assignments we'd gather in conference rooms to trade tips on furthering our careers, complain about our apartments, argue about movies, philosophize about sex, play word games and flirt, often while feasting on Chinese food that lawyers had left behind.

Night paralegal Dan Elish became my first New York BFF pretty much the instant I heard him reciting the lyrics of the *Mister Ed* theme song as though spoken by King Lear. A Mets fan/Knicks fan/New York native who knew everything about Broadway, Dan amazed me when he said he was writing a musical. I didn't realize people were still doing that. In Drama School nobody thought of musicals as art; we didn't write them or study them or even talk about them. But when Dan took me to his seminar at the BMI Musical Theater Workshop one night I found a whole sub-culture of composers, lyricists, and musical book writers who were as inspired to create for the stage as I was. One team at a time presented an excerpt from their latest project to a panel of musical theater legends the likes of the composers of *Annie* and *Godspell*, and the Chief Drama Critic of the *New York Times*, Frank Rich himself. The projects were all smart and delightful. The legends responded with instructions for how to destroy and rebuild the projects so they'd be more smart and delightful. The presenters listened patiently and smiled and said thank you thank you and got back to work using the traditions of yesterday to create the musical theater of tomorrow.

My first New York apartment was in Hell's kitchen in a four-story walk-up where different illegal drugs were sold on every floor. The door to the apartment had two locks and a chain along with a poll brace to prevent customers who found themselves a few dollars short from breaking down the door. I lived there with actor/playwright/comedian/juggler David Garfield whom I hardly ever saw since his money job went from midnight until dawn, and it's lucky that our schedules were out of synch because two people couldn't be awake in that tiny apartment at the same time without having discourse or intercourse. David's room was a nook in the back, and there was a narrow kitchen/hallway leading to the prison-cell-sized common room where I slept on a fold out couch made of sponge. I'd get home from Skadden at 3 AM, sleep until 10, go for a run, shower, head out to the library to write, then walk across town to work as the sun set, grabbing slices of pizza and power bars along the way.

On nights I wasn't working I went out to see shows by myself so I could choose the exact adventure I felt like in the moment. There were realistic plays and classic musicals, but I'd seen all that. I wanted to find shows that would shake up my head, and what a variety of mind-opening stuff there was to see in New

York in the early 80s. I saw a sexual circus play, a punk soap opera, a performance piece in which actors interacted with filmed versions of themselves, a collaboration between a famous avant-garde director and a porn star, a dream play about death in Polish, a high-speed version of *The Crucible* with puppets, aerial dance, punk ballet, topless women painted gold writhing in cages, and brand new plays by my favorite rule-breakers: Irene Fornez, Sam Shepard, Franz Kroetz, Dario Fo, and Samuel Beckett. I also saw centuries-old art forms that were brand new to me, like Kabuki theater, Chinese opera, and ritual dance from around the world. These theatrical events were my real drama school. They showed me how it was possible to go a million miles away from realism to capture reality. And tickets were usually cheap. If a show cost more than fifteen dollars per seat I could get standing room, partial view, an extra ticket some nice person was willing to give away to a young man with big eyes, or I could usher to see the show for free. Occasionally I'd go to the TKTS booth for a half price ticket to a Broadway show; the theatrical palaces of Broadway were a few-minutes walk from my door.

LESSON: See everything.

I took a million mile journey from realism one Friday night when I walked nine blocks up to the Metropolitan Opera and got a standing room ticket for that evening's performance which happened to be *La Boheme*. From way up in the back of the theater I could see the lavish set by Franco Zeffirelli and make out tiny figurines moving around on it. The figurines were singing in Italian and this was before super-title translations so I had no idea what they were saying, but Puccini's music gave me everything I needed: that feeling of being poor at the holidays but you feel great because you're with your friends, the sudden rush of going from stuck to flying when you meet someone with pretty eyes.

The operatic style of singing I'd found annoying on my Dad's records made perfect sense now; the performers used their powerful, precise vibratos to reach me and draw me into the drama. I was right there with the lovers as they struggled to get along, endured that awful break up neither really wanted, and came rushing back together for that long last goodbye. In standing room I could sway and clench my fists, or step back and conduct without hitting anybody. How could you sit still through something that intense anyway? When the lights came up three thousand people screamed and stomped and cheered for minutes before heading out into the cold New York night feeling warm.

I returned to the Met to see if other operas were that good. They were. And there was a different one every night. Each time I discovered a new favorite opera I'd come back to hear it again and again like it was a new Joni Mitchell album. I couldn't get enough of Mozart's *Marriage of Figaro*. How could anything be that hilarious and gorgeous at the same time? I enjoyed Puccini's other operas, but when I got into Verdi's last four masterpieces I thought opera couldn't get better than that. Then I found Wagner. In the middle of his career Wagner created a new form of music-drama that's like a drug-induced spiritual trip. Sometimes he slows things way down so you hear a simple triad, or even a single note, as though you've never heard one before. His operas made me feel like I was experiencing time and space and the far-out beauty of being alive in our boundless universe for the first time. There were a few modern operas that I had to see over and over again, like *Porgy and Bess*, *The Rise and Fall of the City of Mahagonny*, *Wozzeck*, *Pelleas and Melisandre*, and *Einstein on the Beach*, each of which combines music and drama with such originality that it's like the creators have come up with a whole new art form.

As for my own scripts, they were failures of just the right kind. Inspired by all I'd seen I tried out new theatrical styles, pushed everything to extremes, wrote and revised until I loved every word and felt certain the play was perfect. Soon after finishing

I'd be on my morning run and it would strike me that the play I'd just finished didn't work at all. Since I wasn't playing it safe to avoid upsetting professors, the problems in my scripts were big and obvious so I could spot what I'd done wrong easily, learn from my errors, and move on. My experiments were more about style than substance at first. But after a year my writing gained some weight, as my focus shifted from things happening inside theaters to outside, on the sidewalks of New York.

As President Reagan's cuts to social programs took effect in the mid-1980s, more and more people were left without homes. On nearly every block you'd see people lying on pieces of card-board, crouched on subway grates for heat, or standing there asking for help; the ones with confused looks on their faces always made me think of my brother.

As the poor got poorer, greed became fashionable. It wasn't just the corporate lawyers working around the clock on mergers and acquisitions, or the Wall Street traders who made those big deals possible with their junk bonds, or the super rich CEOs who followed their merging and acquiring with massive layoffs politely called "downsizing", in the 80s everybody wanted more more more. Madonna may have meant "Material Girl" ironically, but nobody took it that way; it became the unofficial theme song of my generation. A young upwardly mobile professional (yuppy) was considered a good catch. A sensitive artist was not. Meanwhile, Reagan was reelected in a landslide carrying even New York State.

While the Reagan administration ignored the onset of AIDS, those of us in the New York arts community couldn't. Two months after meeting with a big deal theater agent I called to check in and learned that he was "deceased". A legendary down-town director was too depressed to meet with me because the stage manager he'd worked with for decades had died and four actors in his company were dying. Three actors from a profes-sional production of *Three Sisters* that had been done at Princeton when I was there all died within a month of one another. And then it started happening to my friends. Classmates from drama school and college were becoming sick and weak and dying in their twenties. It made no sense.

I had to do something with all that, but when I tried to focus my writing on serious 80s themes the writing was general and generic and boring. I had no idea how to translate what was going on in the streets to a dramatic form that was personal.

Then one day the outer world made its way into my gut. As I was having my daily slice at a pizza place on the corner of Eighth Avenue and 51st street:

*A small man with a scar on his lip asked me to help him get some food for himself and his friend, but the manager chased him out. When I went outside and gave the small man with the scar a dollar he said that he used to work as a spray painter for CBS but there were no more jobs so now "I live in the street with my friend," indicating a man with long white hair hanging down from under a wool cap. I asked where they go when it gets cold. "Wherever we can."

*As I walked down 8th avenue, a short woman in fake fur coat wearing pink high heels hurried along the sidewalk shouting "I'm here hun" to a guy down the block wearing a leather jacket and pushing a baby carriage. The guy turned and frowned at the woman and let her catch up. When they reached a corner he started across, she pointed to the right, they changed course and hurried along as he went ahead of her again.

*Across the street a woman called for help as a crowd gathered around a man lying on the ground. The man was lying still on his back, eyes open. "He cut his tenacles!" the woman shouted. I noticed blood coming from the man's crotch. When a man they called "the super" tried to help the bleeding man up the bleeding man sprung to his feet and ran around trying to punch people. I headed towards a payphone to call an ambulance but just before I called one arrived, medics bound and bandaged the bleeding man and took him away, leaving only his bloody pants and worn shoes on the sidewalk.

*A tiny woman asked me to help her cross the street because she had gout. As we walked she told me she had fled the USSR during World War Two, her family could only eat bread and water while hiding and "That's why I didn't grow."

*A woman with a scar on her lip asked me for a dollar. After I gave it to her she asked if I wanted "some fun". When I declined she told me she'd taken her daughter to see *Sesame Street Live* over the weekend and that she lived on 150th street, "the nice part of Harlem."

*A bus went by with a sign that said *NOISES OFF!* "I DIDN'T WANT TO LEAVE THE THEATER!"

*A man with no legs sat on a director's chair shaking a can.

*I ran into someone I knew from college who told me that our director friend Katherine had lupus but it was in remission, and that he was on his way to see his girlfriend Wendy.

All these unrelated events added up to something for me. I felt intoxicated and dizzy, like I was about to laugh or cry but I couldn't tell which. The world seemed a schizoid circus that exists beyond dichotomies of happy/sad, funny/serious, sane/insane, normal/weird, grand/grotesque. Along with mental illness, mutilation, poverty, and hunger there was vigor, a spirit of survival, friends and strangers coming together to help each other. In this context the bus sign was funnier than anything in the farce it advertised.

LESSON: To see the world, stop and look at it.

After my walk down Eighth Avenue I set out to capture the everything-at-once feeling in my plays as though guided by a manifesto:

*Life is a comedic sketch with a serious punch line.

*Nothing matters except everything.

*Funny and serious are everywhere every second you're on earth.

*A mixed up picture of the world strikes me as true and turns me on.

*The mess itself is the beauty.

In response to what I'd seen on my walk I wrote a series of street scenes; the focus on greed, disease, poverty, and the threat of war made this play more compelling than my earlier writing, and funnier.

LESSON: Don't try to be funny or weird. See the funny weirdness and express it.

With high hopes I passed the script to every theater I knew, using a strategy I developed while dating:

LESSON: Passionate good, desperate bad.

When introducing yourself to the theater's literary department, make it clear that you love what they're doing, mentioning a specific show or shows. But never act like a beggar. Remember: They need good plays. Without good plays they have no theater. Instead of saying to yourself: "I'm so lucky you're even acknowledging my existence," convince yourself that: "Someone will produce this play. Sure it would be great for me if you produce it, but it would be great for you too." It's okay to check in a couple months later to make sure the script hasn't gotten lost, but don't nag. You're not desperate, you're busy.

Of course, I was desperate. I tried to tell people about my walk down Eighth Avenue at parties, at work, on dates, but as I heard the words coming out of my head it all sounded silly, my passion made no sense and made listeners feel awkward.

LESSON: As a playwright you spend most of your life in the vast gap between saying something and being heard.

Revved up for connection I went looking for women to hold, scared them all away. I went to shows alone, always alone, where I'd laugh too much, cheer too much, whisper curses at this trite bullshit, cry quietly in the dark, or give a standing ovation even if nobody else was standing. The hardest part of going to the theater was in the beginning when the lights came up; I always felt sad that it wasn't my play being performed.

Eventually the rejection letters started coming in – but also a great phone call from a great theater. Tim Sanford, the scholarly literary manager at Playwrights Horizons, wanted to do a reading of my play for artistic director Andre Bishop. As cool as his name, Andre Bishop had made Playwrights Horizons the go-to place for sharp new comedies by people like Christopher Durang and Wendy Wasserstein. The Playwrights Horizons casting department got amazing actors and the reading was perfect – well it sounded perfect, my eyes were closed the whole time.

Afterwards Andre Bishop invited me to meet with him. When he asked why I was interested in writing for the stage as opposed to TV or film I drew a total blank, eventually muttered something about language. Andre told me he was interested in work that was original and crisp that could appeal to the wider public; he didn't want to do plays "in a basement somewhere." Then Andre said nice things about my writing and finished with: "I'm sure we'll be working together some day." Those words from Andre Bishop! I couldn't wait to go outside and dance with them. *The New York Times* reviewed everything at Playwrights Horizons, and if the *Times* got excited about the play it could have an extended run or move to a bigger theater, maybe even on Broadway, and theaters across the country would do the play and then ask for my next play and my next -- I was a couple ifs and a some day away from a sweet career.

A year later I was back at Playwrights Horizons with my next play, which I felt was my ultimate masterpiece. After it was presented in a reading I waited for a Yes Let's Do it from Andre through Tim. But instead of a Yes or a No I got a Maybe. Five other theaters did readings of the play, responded with a series of enthusiastic Maybes. Months passed. No movement on the Maybes. I had time to write another new play, but did I really want to spend another year of private time with my computer in return for a bunch more Maybes?

After a performance of *La Boheme* I'd been struck by the contrast between the lush world of Puccini's young artists and the harshness of mine, as I passed people dying on the sidewalk on the way to my drug-infested building. When I tried to write a play based on *Boheme* set in modern New York I couldn't get my young artist characters to talk. But when I imagined the story with music it seemed that the anger and love could pour out of them. If I pursued my updated *Boheme* as a musical project -- not a traditional musical, but something as unique as those modern operas I loved -- I could have a new kind of adventure, try to interest a different set of producers, maybe get more than a Maybe.

CHAPTER 5.

HOW NOT TO COLLABORATE

One head taking in the world, seeing things from its own perspective, coming up with a way to express what it sees in its own idiosyncratic way, I get that. But two different heads, each with its own way of seeing things, coming together to create one pure original thing? How is that possible?

In the fall of 1988 I needed it to be possible, since I wanted to write a musical but don't compose music. When I asked Ira Weitzman, the head of musical theater at Playwrights Horizons, if he could recommend a composer to supply an original noisy sound for my *Boheme*, he got back to me with two names:

1) Jonathan Larson, whose rock musical *Superbia* had been performed in staged readings and won a prize, and

2) Adam Guettel, whom Ira described as young (he was 25, Jonathan almost 30), probably a genius, and the grandson of Richard Rodgers.

When I invited Adam over for lunch I was living in the West Village so I could go around the corner to pick up a loaf of New York's best Italian bread from Zito's bakery (Sinatra had a loaf flown to him every morning) and shop at my favorite specialty shops on Bleecker Street for the finest meats, cheeses, and toppings. When Adam showed up I described myself as a playwright obsessed with music and he said he was a composer who had a similar obsession with drama. I told him I admired traditional musicals but wanted to do something different. He felt the same way. We discussed music, theater, opera, movies...At some point Adam interrupted the conversation to say, "This is an amazing sandwich." He was humble, handsome, easy to talk to, smart, and thoughtful. How could you not love this guy?

After we exchanged materials and Adam headed out, I put his cassette into my player and listened to "Icarus", a 5-minute pop opera about flying up to the sun, followed by an impressionistic response to a Chekov story, a rock song about raunchy sex, a jingle for a typewriter commercial...Everything on Adam's tape was fascinating. When I called him to say how much I loved his work and describe my *Boheme* idea, Adam said he wasn't interested in doing something contemporary; there were a few specific historical periods that interested him at the time. I was sorry not to be on Adam Guettel's path to glory, but honored that he met with me and liked my sandwich.

In my first phone call with Jonathan Larson he described his music as "really good FM rock" and said his enemy was the shallow, glossy culture of the day epitomized by music videos and Madonna. After we exchanged materials Jonathan mentioned the possibility of adapting *The Suicide*, a Soviet farce about how a pointless death can take on super-powerful meaning. I pitched him *Boheme* and also said we could do an over-the-top rock satire; the futuristic setting and muscular rock songs from Jonathan's *Superbia* made me think of my beloved *Rocky Horror Picture Show*. But from the moment Jonathan heard about my *Boheme* idea, that's what he wanted to do. He felt the linking of opera to rock gave it "high-brow and low-brow appeal", and that it was exactly right for our times.

When we met at his place in the way-west Village to get to work, Jonathan led me up a ladder to the rooftop where he held meetings and offered me a choice of beach chairs. I didn't have a comfortable rapport with Jonathan the way I did with Adam, so after minimal small talk we got down to business. After I talked Jonathan through the four-part structure of the opera's story and explained how we could use it as a framework, he suggested we set the show in the East Village where the bohemians of New York could still afford to live. He went on to talk about the story in terms of good people who were making art and everybody else who was selling out, and envisioned an angry song aimed at commercial producers who make lush Broadway musicals. As Jonathan's collaborator I should have explained why I hadn't imagined the show focusing on a particular neighborhood, and told him I wasn't comfortable suggesting that artists were better than other people or that trying to make money is evil. Unfortunately I suck at expressing the slightest disagreement on the spot and am much better at keeping my feelings to myself and writing about them 37 years later.

LESSON: Don't aim to please your collaborator at all costs as you might a guest at your party, or humor your collaborator as you would your grandmother.

LESSON: Be totally honest with your collaborator right from the beginning.

LESSON: Make sure you share a vision of the project before committing to working together.

Jonathan seemed shy and nervous in my company but strong willed at the same time. He was tall, his hair stuck out from the top of his head, his ears stuck out and his feelings stuck out. Even when Jonathan was quiet I could sense his restlessness to make something happen. It didn't matter how poor this guy was, how many years he'd been waiting tables, or the fact that he'd never had a show produced, he believed he was going all the way and never stopped swinging for the fences. With complete confidence Jonathan told me that our *Boheme* would be our generation's *Hair* and bring the MTV generation back to the theater. I thought he was nuts, but in a good way.

As the word guy in our collaboration it was up to me to go first. But when I sat down to write the script I found that my head was no longer my own...I was sharing it with a collaborator. With Jonathan's voice and mine telling me what to write at the same time, I couldn't hear a thing. I don't believe in writer's block. When what's inside you is good you can't wait to write it down. If you don't feel like writing, it usually means there's some sort of contradiction that needs to be worked out. So when I'm stumped I put the project aside to get perspective. But when Jonathan called a couple times to remind me how anxious he was for something to work on, I pushed myself to keep going, forced the characters to talk through the first scene, and passed Jonathan the result.

When you find someone to collaborate with there's a rush of elation. Suddenly you have access to new skills. New contacts too, and new credits to brag about at parties. But as you get to work you realize a terrible fact:

LESSON: The other person isn't you.

Some things your collaborator contributes won't be what you had in mind at all because your collaborator doesn't have the exact same tastes, values, intuitions, sense of humor, education, and parents as you. And so begins the slow work of collaboration. With respect and humility, you have to explain how you think your collaborator's work could be improved, and listen patiently with an open mind as they respond. Jonathan and I had no idea how to do any of that. We were a pair of headstrong artists used to having total control, more comfortable taking turns doing things our own way than actually working together.

When Jonathan called to talk about the pages I'd sent to give us something to talk about, we had nothing to talk about. Jonathan's response was blunt: "There's nothing there that couldn't be in *Thirty Something*." *Thirty Something* was a well constructed, ground breaking TV show that was popular at the time, but to us it symbolized yuppy escapism. Understanding his comment as a personal attack I responded in kind, "The characters in *Thirty Something* would love your music." So mean.

We stumbled into an actual conversation when Jonathan brought up *Do the Right Thing* as an example of a strong, original, angry creation by someone from our generation. We agreed on that, so Spike Lee's film gave me a point of focus. When Jonathan reminded me "I want something to work on" I told him I get it, but the script has to come from inside me and I can't rush so please no pressure. He said fine.

As soon as Jonathan gave me permission to take whatever time I needed I didn't need any time. I imagined a playwright and painter wearing black in an utterly un-luscious anti-Puccini world. They're confused, angry, hungry and frozen. Their parents don't get them. Nobody wants their work. The stressed playwright chants in long lines of stressed syllables punctuated by a staccato sentence: Rent. The painter does the same and then, again: Rent. After a two-line interchange they have a one-line chorus: How are we gonna pay this month's rent.

As these two finish their rant, their philosopher roommate sings that they should stop beating themselves up and open up a restaurant in Santa Fe. When I had visited Santa Fe a couple years earlier it seemed like New York in an alternate universe... an arts community with a slow pace, plenty of space, and clean air. In times of stress I used to fantasize about opening a restaurant there with my Yale philosopher friend Larry who was wrestling with an intractable PhD thesis on Heidegger, and high school friend Daniel whose graduate work at Columbia had him screaming in his sleep and wearing a mouth guard to keep him from grinding his teeth while studying. Inspired by Larry's charming volubility, I gave the philosopher character a sly, laid-back way of expressing himself.

When the lovers meet and merge in Puccini's opera they express their feelings with pure unbounded joy. In anti-Puccini land Playwright and Mimi begin awkwardly, singing "I should tell you" back and forth without telling anything. Observing late 80s etiquette, they get to their sexual history right away and open up about past disasters and fears. A series of broken phrases passes between them before they let go and slide into a kind of dream together, still tentative, asleep on pins. Then they go out into the who-knows-where holding hands. End of Act 1.

Jonathan loved what I'd written, all of it, every word. He loved that the characters said fuck and shit. He loved the anger in the opening song "Rent" which he felt would "blow the audience out of their seats" and said we should make that menacing R-word the title of the show. He told me to keep going so I wrote more lyrics and he loved those too. Between Jonathan and me it was either YES YES YES or NO NO NO. More nuanced communication would have served us well but being on the receiving end of the yesses felt great.

Then it was Jonathan's turn to get to work and mine to wait anxiously. After a while I checked in to learn that he'd already completed music for "Rent" and "Santa Fe", but the ballad "I Should Tell You" was taking forever. When he finally had me over to hear the songs Jonathan said he was nervous and I could tell he was. As he played the opening riff in the song "Rent" on his cheap electric keyboard I got nervous too. That little keyboard didn't have much bass, so the driving dissonant rock number sounded clinky and cartoony; it made me think of a bunch of marching cartoon ants. For a few seconds that felt like forever I sat there wondering what I could possibly say to this guy who was pouring his heart into a song about angry ants that he thought would change the musical theater. Keeping up my smile was a struggle until he reached the chorus with its repeated question about paying the rent and I got the sense of swelling anger he was going for. I relaxed, imagined more bass, and trusted his talent. The next song "Santa Fe" I got right away; the smooth music perfectly matched the feel of the lyrics and I loved the repeating bass riff. Then came "I Should Tell You" which I thought was incredible. He'd caught the scary thrill of discovering another person by using queasy half steps up and down to create the feeling of uncertain ground. And when the lovers got through the awkward interchange his music sent them soaring off together, free. I thought "I Should Tell You" was about a hundred times better than anything I'd heard from *Superbia*. When I told Jonathan I loved the songs he exhaled and said, "We have something to work on."

For our next step, Jonathan said we should spend a few hundred bucks to make a tape of the songs to pass to theaters. That caught me off guard; I never expected to make money with my plays but sure didn't want to lose any. Our expense doubled as Jonathan used the new technique of sampling to record the instruments, which he assured me was the way to go. When it was time to record the voices Jonathan called in his talented friends: Roger Bart hit awesome high notes as the playwright, bass/baritone John Cavaluzzo sang the philosopher beautifully, Valarie Pettiford was a powerful Mimi, and Jonathan sang Mark himself. Afterwards he kept editing and polishing the tape and let me know that the cost had gone up again. When I balked Jonathan said it was too late, this is how we're doing it, but don't worry you'll love the tape. In the end my share of the cost for that tape of 3 songs was around 600 dollars. There were entire months I didn't make 600 dollars. But I forgave Jonathan for the expense when I got the tape; I couldn't stop listening to it.

When Jonathan passed the tape to producers along with a script they didn't get the show. Jonathan asked me to write a story outline we could send out with the tape instead of the script, but still no interest. We loved our project so much, but nobody loved it back. It was time for Jonathan and me to have an honest discussion about why people weren't getting the piece, exactly what we wanted it to be, and what needed to be done next to get it there. But in our tradition of not actually collaborating we never had that conversation.

I began writing a series of satirical short plays for adults based on Grimm's fairy tales and Jonathan moved on to *Boho Days*, his solo show that would later be called *Tick Tick Boom!* In this musical about Jonathan's life as a struggling artist he dealt with his anger at commercial culture and other themes from *Rent* in just the way he wanted. Besides writing all the music and words Jonathan played all the roles himself, keeping collaboration to an absolute minimum. When I came to see his show Jonathan and I shared a big hug and he said we should talk some more about *Rent*.

Back on his rooftop a week later, Jonathan told me he felt that both *Rent* and *Boho Days* hadn't gone far enough. What if lots of the characters in *Rent* had AIDS, they were all really poor, and some were addicted to heroine. I told him it sounded great but that I didn't know people who did heroine and wasn't sure I could write those characters in a way that would be vivid rather than generic. So Jonathan said he'd set up a meeting for us with his friend Max Cantor who wrote about East Village drug culture for the *Village Voice*. I didn't hear from Jonathan for a while, and when he finally called it was to ask if he could go ahead with *Rent* on his own. He didn't mention the meeting with Max, and I didn't ask about it. I've since learned that Max Cantor was found dead with a needle in his arm Oct 3, 1991, the day before I got that call from Jonathan. Whether Max's death had anything to do with Jonathan's decision, the fact is that Jonathan had a clear idea of what he wanted to do with the show and I had a lot else going on and was glad to let go of our prickly collaboration.

LESSON: It can be harder to collaborate on a musical than a marriage.

When I moved into a Brooklyn apartment with my fiancée Lisa Vogel (sister of philosopher friend Larry), Lisa cared about couches and I cared about stereo speakers so she chose the couches and I chose the speakers. But in a musical the script and music have to support each other always, both collaborators have to love every word and every note.

In the end, there was one aspect of collaboration Jonathan and I got exactly right:

LESSON: When talking money with your collaborator, get it in writing.

We agreed, in a letter we both signed, that Jonathan could go ahead with the show on his own, and that if Rent ever got produced I'd get credit for "original concept and additional lyrics" as well as compensation.

After my tense collaboration with Jonathan I was once again free to do my own thing, follow impulses I couldn't put into words, put a piece aside if I wasn't getting it, and make major changes in a script without explaining myself.

Meanwhile my romantic collaboration was going great. When Lisa and I got married, a life-long friend gave a toast in which he said I was a genius.

LESSON: When an artist is getting married, be sure to have someone give a toast saying that the artist is a genius, since most of the guests are quietly wondering if the groom/bride will ever make a living.

A few months before the wedding, when Lisa and I moved in together I'd had a writer's typical fears:

1.What if we're both home, I'm writing down an idea for a scene, and she starts talking to me?

And:

2. What if we're going for a walk, I'm developing an idea in my head, and she starts talking to me?

But fairly quickly I came to see that:

LESSON: When you're home with your romantic partner it's not like having a friend you have to entertain, you can each do your own thing, ignoring each other all day, and it's fine.

And:

LESSON: When going for walks with your partner it's not a date, you can just look at things in silence or you can converse with your partner like a normal person instead of searching for artistic inspiration now and then, it's really not that hard.

A bigger concern that took longer to acknowledge and address: 3. What if you start yelling at each other to go to hell and breaking each other's stuff and suing each other and wind up having to live apart from your own kids? I don't know what percentage of artists grew up with unhappily-married parents but the good news for all of us is:

LESSON: You're not your parents.

Living with my calm, cheerful, mentally stable wife, I came to see that:

LESSON: As long as you can listen to each other and talk to each other, you and your partner can get through anything.

When I realized it was working out between Lisa and me, I felt so happy.

LESSON: Even the most in-your-head artist, with a history of depression and divorced parents and a future of question marks, can find true love.

I would still go out alone and look at all the people going by, notice their faces, observe the way they moved and the clusters they formed. But when I was out with beautiful Lisa I wanted people to look at me.

※ ※ ※

CHAPTER 6.

LEARNING TO USE YOUR TALENT TO MAKE MONEY

After a year and a half of marriage I found myself in a hospital holding a brand new 7 pound human wrapped in a blanket, my boy Jake. Two years later I brought Jake back to the hospital to meet his new baby sister, Anna. After holding the baby in his lap, being extra careful with the head, Jake gave her back to Lisa and asked, "Who's its mommy?" "I am." "Who's its daddy?" "I am." We'd explained all this, but the new normal was just now sinking in for Jake, and for me. Though Lisa and I shared expenses, with her stable job doing immigration work at NYU she knew exactly what she'd be making from week to week. I had no idea.

At this point I'd left Skadden and was writing parody videos for a Wall Street investment bank on a freelance basis. The main thing I learned from writing parody videos was:

LESSON: Work that uses your super power will pay more than work that doesn't.

In other words:

LESSON: You can use your artistic skills to make good money.

After getting the check for my first parody video I was finally able to buy a VCR (with hifi stereo sound!). Now that we'd need a bigger living space, more food, more everything, I decided to put playwriting aside for a while and focus on getting as many money gigs as I could.

My first step was to scan the 63 cable channels on TV (which at the time felt like an insane number) to see what was out there.

LESSON: If you want to work for TV, see what's on TV.

Every time I found a show I thought I could write for, I contacted the producer, gushed about what I'd just seen, then submitted my resume and writing samples with a cover letter explaining how my entire life prepared me to write for this particular show. I used the same approach when applying to producers of radio shows, home videos, computer games, audio tapes, CD/Roms, and live entertainment for corporate events.

The first gigs I was offered were small, let's-see-how-it-goes kind of deals, but I always said yes. No matter how much I hated the work I'd get through it, and get right back to contacting producers and gushing and submitting.

A note about gushing: You have to mean it.

LESSON: Fill your gush with specific details about the show.

When I was producing a TV show myself I was constantly getting emails from writers who didn't seem to have any particular interest in our show; it was like they'd typed the show's name into a form letter. They were wasting my time. If a show is on TV, it already has writers. You need to give producers a clue that you might be better than the people they've already got. Your genuine love of the show is a clue.

LESSON: If you can't find a way to enjoy what you're writing, the client won't enjoy it either.

When I auditioned to write for the soap opera *General Hospital* I was sent a pack of scripts, outlines, and story lines for the show covering the last several years and the next few months, and a scene-by-scene outline of the episode they wanted me to write. I couldn't get over how carefully the writers structured the story over the course of a season, and broke it down with precision so that tension would build over every episode and every week would end with a "cliff-hanger" compelling viewers to come back Monday. There's a ton to learn about dramatic storytelling from the soaps, but the main thing I learned is: You can't just connect the dots and collect checks. Successful soap writers have fun being inventive within the story structure and delight in bringing those characters to life. Though I studied all the materials, watched many episodes, and devoted myself to the *General Hospital* audition script, I couldn't relate to the characters well enough to make them feel alive so the writing didn't flow, and I didn't get the job.

LESSON: Your most successful money gigs will tap into your natural talent.

Though writing TV drama for adults was a challenge, while writing for slop-and-slime-happy early Nickelodeon shows I found that kid stuff came naturally to me. *Turkey TV* and *Don't Just Sit There!* paid 100 dollars per goopy skit, so I could write 4 in a day and feel rich. For PBS's game show *Where in the World is Carmen Sandiego* I wrote goofy fact-filled text, then I wrote an episode for PBS's kinder gentler *Reading Rainbow. Rainbow* paid well for a reason: the producers made you do five drafts of the script and requested specific word changes line by line after every draft. By the end of the process the producers had written my script.

LESSON: In TV they can change every word you write.
But that was okay. The producers got what they wanted and I got paid so everybody was happy.

LESSON: Be nice to people who reject you.

When I applied to write for shows at Children's Television Workshop (now Sesame Workshop) I was always rejected. At one point I checked in with a CTW producer to see about upcoming possible gigs, she had nothing, but recommended me to free-lance producer Joanne Roberts.

LESSON: When people ask for ideas, have some.

Joanne was looking for new show ideas so I pitched her *President Phoebe*, an educational show about how government works that featured a kid president supported by a staff of her best friends in a White House inspired by *Pee Wee's Playhouse*. Joanne liked the idea, took *President Phoebe* to CTW where it was optioned. In search of a network to team up with, CTW brought *President Phoebe* to NBC. One NBC producer after another liked the idea and passed it up to her superior until the very top guy said yes let's do it, but a kid president is "unbelievable" so make her Governor Phoebe.

LESSON: TV networks are desperate for something different but when they get something different they take away the thing that made it different.

As we developed *Governor Phoebe* the NBC guy who made us demote Phoebe didn't like the show any more, maybe because it was still "unbelievable" but now without the fun of having a country ruled by kids in a fantastical White House. So CTW took *Governor Phoebe* to producers at ABC who liked it and ordered a pilot script. Since I didn't have network TV writing experience, other writers were hired to write the script.

LESSON: In television they can replace you on your own project.
As normal writers wrote the script for my abnormal idea, ABC came to feel the same way I did about a kid governor and let the project go. Eventually Phoebe was demoted to "Citizen Phoebe" and featured in a series of interstitials on Noggin, a network that no longer exists.

Though Phoebe never made it to the White House, I was paid at every step.

LESSON: When making a development deal, have a lawyer.
Reading the first draft of the contract between Joanne and CTW and me gave me a stomach cramp. I had no idea what I was actually promising to do and whether the amounts I was offered were fair. So I hired an arts lawyer who handled negotiations beautifully and made sure I'd get paid at every stage of the

development/destruction of *Phoebe*. Since lawyers charge by the hour, hiring one on a project that might never make a cent is a risk; but I see the lawyer's fee as an investment in your career. You're worth it. If you can't afford a lawyer there are groups like Volunteer Lawyers for the Arts that can help you out for little or nothing.

LESSON: Use every money job to get more.

As I added my kids TV credits to my resume I was able to get work writing for kids magazines and TV show spinoff books. Since *Carmen Sandiego* was a game show I was able to use that credit to get work writing for a VH1 game show, which led to writing promos for VH1, Cartoon Network, MTV...

LESSON: Eventually, clients call YOU.

When *Beavis and Butthead* showed up on MTV people either loved it or hated it. While some of the rough early episodes seem mean-spirited, I found the show hilarious and true. As an adolescent boy you're obsessed with sex but your body is repulsive so you hang out with a friend and make stupid jokes. When I got a call asking if I wanted to write for the show I came back with a barrage of ideas, they hired me to write a bunch, ended up a making a few, the best of which was the one in which Beavis mistakes his constipation for pregnancy. *Beavis* scripts are short, and half the time you're typing "Beavis: Huh huh huh! Butt-head: Huh huh huh huh huh!" But the huhs have to be carefully placed, set up, and earned, and surrounded by words that aren't huh.

LESSON: There are true artists working in television.

Mike Judge's crudely animated *Beavis and Butt-head* was both the weirdest and most realistic thing on TV. A few years later, another creator pulled off a similarly impressive feat in his own freaky style. When I was invited to write for John Dilworth's cult Cartoon Network hit *Courage the Cowardly Dog* I didn't get the whimsical creepiness...until I realized that all the scary stuff Courage sees is based on something that terrifies John Dilworth about our world. In one episode Courage's master the Farmer takes his massive rifle out to shoot a deer and finds a deer with a more massive rifle hunting *him*; in another episode a deranged Snowman seeks revenge on humans for melting his home in the North Pole. The meetings at which the stories were created were as wild as the stories themselves. As the head writer tried to lead a room of writers and consultants towards a complete story, John would shout out ideas for visuals, bizarre plot twists, and self-referential gags...But how to get there? And where to go next? Soon everybody was throwing out ideas as the episode writer (me) tried desperately to get it all down. Behind all that madness was a courageous artist, who, like his hero Courage, saw everything.

LESSON: Stay in touch with your money gig friends.

After a few years of TV writing I found myself in an informal community of freelance friends with whom I could share info such as:

*How much $ can you ask for?

*Will the notes be useful or random or stupid or vague or insulting?

*Will they ask you to make changes in a draft and still call it the same draft so the agreed to two-drafts-and-a-polish will actually be too-many-drafts-to-count dragging on for months?

*Will the client ever pay you or say they couldn't use what you'd written and offer a kill fee or claim they've run out of money and offer apologies or say your bill is an outrage and stop taking your calls?

Yes all those things happened to me. A lot. But in spite of all the horrors of freelance work, the main thing we'd ask each other was:

*Who's hiring?

When a busy funny-writer pal couldn't take a job at Comedy Central he recommended me for the gig and I got it – writing for Short Attention Span Theater.

LESSON: My funny might not be your funny.
The show host was up-and-coming comedian Marc Maron, whose brilliant, dark wit didn't go well with my semi-sweet wit. As I tried to write jokes for Marc I realized I don't like writing jokes. I don't even like jokes.

LESSON: In search of money, you might find love.

The biggest surprise in my writing-for-money career was how much I love educational writing. In my audition to write a science module for third graders, I was asked to write a chapter about How Birds Fly following these rules:

LESSON: Sentences should flow smoothly from one to the next.

LESSON: Supporting examples should be concrete and clear.

LESSON: Text should convey a sense of why the reader should care.

These simple, beautiful rules work for playwriting too, where dramatic beats are your sentences, scenes are supporting examples, and you have to make your audience care about the story or all is lost. But with educational writing the content is factual, which I found refreshing. Instead of digging deep inside yourself for answers, you can get them from a library. Whether you're writing for textbooks or kids magazines or documentary films, the work is objective, addresses an obvious need, and you get paid.

LESSON: Like making art, making money with your talent takes imagination and resilience.

As you search for clients think outside the box, put your heart into every assignment, when you get rejected get back up, and keep on pushing.

As money projects became full time I continued to fantasize about plays, but wouldn't let myself write a new one unless there was some reason to think the next play would be better than the others -- or at least different in a way that would open new doors. Instead of going into town to see plays, I'd read Frank Rich's dismissive reviews and try to convince myself the theater was dead. Hearing that a friend's play was getting produced would ruin my day. Another thing that could ruin my day: Those rows of books in the library called *Best Plays. Best Comedies. Best Short Plays. Best New American Plays.* How could they be so sure those were *Best* plays, if they don't know *my* plays?

LESSON: When feeling small, act big.

When I sent my one-act adult version of "Little Red Riding Hood" to the editor of the short plays series he chose it for *Best American Short Plays 92-93.* Suddenly infatuated with all things Best, I used my author's discount to buy dozens of copies and distributed them to everyone I knew. The best thing I discovered from my Best experience was that there are amateur theater groups all over the country and beyond looking for new plays. Over the next couple years my "Little Red" was performed by theaters with names like Renegades in Heat in Greeley, Colorado; the Unsafe Ensemble in Davenport, Iowa; the Prospero Acting Group in Hvammstangi, Iceland; Hell's Kitchen Sink at EST in New York; the Bisbee Rep in Bisbee, Arizona; and the Armadillo Theater in Athens, Greece. Since people were making use of my last play, I allowed myself to write a new one. The potential energy that had been building up in my brain converted to kinetic and the writing flowed.

LESSON: If you put your art aside for money, your art will be there when you get back.

❊ ❊ ❊

CHAPTER 7:
LEARNING ABOUT FAME

After Jonathan Larson and I stopped working together on *Rent* he kept me up on his progress, inviting me to readings and sending new material for feedback. I got to hear "Will you Light My Candle", "Will I", and "No Day But Today" for the first time on a cassette tape he sent me after about a year of working on his own, and I enjoyed meeting Angel and a whole community of artists in his ever-expanding script. Jonathan was up to something good and getting better all the time and he knew it. Before passing me that cassette and script he had me sign a second, more explicit statement that the show would always be called "RENT a rock opera by Jonathan Larson. Original concept and additional lyrics by Billy Aronson."

In the fall of 1994 Jonathan invited me to a workshop presentation of *Rent* at the New York Theatre Workshop where there was already a buzz about the show. Usually for a low-budget presentation of a work-in-progress you have to struggle to fill the seats with friends. But for this workshop I couldn't get a ticket for the night I wanted, even after explaining my role, because it was sold out. And when I saw the presentation I understood why. The show was long and loud and didn't all add up, but the parts that worked whipped the audience into a frenzy. Afterwards I told Jonathan he'd found a way to put his entire heart into music, to get everything he was feeling onto the stage.

I wasn't at all surprised when New York Theater Workshop announced that they were going to produce *Rent* in their upcoming season, though I was jealous, and nervous about how my role would be perceived. In January one of the papers had a listing of shows to look for in the coming year that described *Rent* mockingly as "A rock *La Boheme*. Awesome, huh?" I was sure critics were going to love the show but mock its one chronic flaw, the original concept.

As previews approached I called Jonathan to discuss my bio for the program, we went back and forth about whether I wrote lyrics for 3 songs or 2 songs since 1 of them had changed a lot, then whether I wrote lyrics for 2 songs or first-draft lyrics for 3 songs...it was annoying, but we came up with some compromise. At the end of the call I asked how the show was going, Jonathan said it was going to be great and I should hurry up and get my complimentary tickets.

A few days later, while working on *Carmen Sandiego* from a studio in Queens, I "beeped in" to my answering machine and heard a message from a composer friend asking if I'd heard the awful news about Jonathan Larson. When I returned the call, my friend told me that Jonathan had had an aortic aneurism and was found dead on his kitchen floor; he had died the night before the first preview of his show.

When Lisa and I came to see the show it felt like we were *in* a show, a tragedy about an artist who dies at the moment his masterpiece is born. Regretting that I'd squabbled with Jonathan about my credits in our final interaction, I checked the program -- but couldn't find my bio anywhere. A *New York Times* article based on an interview with Jonathan hours before he died suggested Jonathan got the idea for *Rent* from a puppet version of *Boheme* he'd seen as a child. The article's complete omission of my role along with my missing bio in the program made me wonder if Jonathan had decided to totally screw me just before he died. So besides grieving for my former collaborator, I was annoyed about the program, upset that no one in the theater knew me, ashamed of having abandoned such a great project, and petrified that my remaining lyrics would ruin the show.

Then the show began and thank God I'd brought my pack of pocket Kleenex. With new songs that were Jonathan's best, this trimmed and tightened version totally worked. Jonathan's wide-open emotional story ideas that I'd found sentimental, simplistic, and melodramatic, felt grounded and true when expressed through his rock anthems. Or maybe *Rent* really was a melodrama after all, in the tradition of those populist 19th century plays with emotive piano music in which the noble poor fight to keep their homes as the evil rich try to throw them into the street, and audiences gasp and hiss and finally cheer as the miraculous ending allows a moment of hope. Whatever this was that was unfolding in front of me, I'd never seen anything like it. In that small space you could feel the love every one of those young actors had for the work and for Jonathan. *Hair* has a nude scene, but in this play everyone on that stage was emotionally naked the whole time, as wide-open, desperate, and obsessed as Jonathan himself. Like their characters, these young actors were fighting through all the shit the world had thrown at them and reaching for something greater than themselves. Lisa was shaken by the performance and so was I. It was a once-in-a-lifetime experience.

The *New York Times* arts section became a shrine to *Rent*, where everybody on its theater staff left glowing offerings. Besides an A++ review from chief critic Ben Brantley, an editorial rave from Frank Rich, and multiple articles about Jonathan and the director and producers, the *Times* gave every single cast member a huge photo and bio. In those days everybody read the newspaper. At my check-up my doctor made small talk about "this thinly disguised version of *La Boheme*". An old friend called asking if I wanted to see this musical based on *La*

Boheme. Passing a pay phone near Rockefeller Center I heard a woman say, "and it's based on *La Boheme*." The whole run of the show sold out immediately. People were going nuts for tickets, friends asked me if I could get them in but I don't think I could have gotten to see it again myself, there was no way to get your body into that theater to see this thing people all over New York were freaking out about. The show was extended and sold out instantly again. I figured the final extension would be the end of all this noise about the show, but when I couldn't sleep one night I surfed through the channels and found critics Michael Feingold (*Village Voice*) and Clive Barnes (*New York Post*) discussing how *Rent* might go to Broadway. Could those ranting characters in black actually wind up in the land of shiny family entertainment? I dug out my letter of agreement with Jonathan about "compensation and credit" and hired entertainment lawyer Jonathan Herzog to approach the Larson family on my behalf.

When the *Times* finally called to interview me about my role in *Rent* I asked if I could call right back. Finally people would know my role in creating this "theatrical comet", as the *Times* had called it. I spent a few frantic minutes calling my Dad and my lawyer, took many deep breaths, and got ready to address the world via the *New York Times*.

The reporter "Tony" sounded like an eager young rock critic so I walked him through the plot of *La Boheme* step by step as he listened politely. Only later did I learn that Tony was in fact classical music scholar Anthony Tomassini, soon to be chief opera critic of the *Times*. One question I stumbled over was whether Jonathan Larson and I were friends. We had come together for professional reasons and never saw each other except to work on the project. On the other hand our collaboration was amicable. We'd come to each other's readings, hugged as theater people do, sent each other the occasional holiday card. So I said we were friends.

If only I'd been friends with Jonathan's family. When Jonathan died his father, mother, and sister inherited artistic control of his work and his income from the show. Understandably, they didn't love the idea of someone they didn't know taking partial credit for the masterpiece to which Jonathan had devoted the last years of his life. So the Larsons' lawyer responded to mine that if I didn't accept their token offer I'd get nothing and the Larsons would remove my contributions from the show. Remove my words from those songs? And how do you remove a show's original concept? My lawyer assured me that this is how people negotiate, and suggested I decline their offer and try to do better if I have the stomach for it. I said yes let's go for it, although in truth I didn't have the stomach for it. Then he told me that the Larsons had asked the *Times* to withhold my interview from the upcoming article about the creation of *Rent*. My poor lawyer had to listen to me rage until I was hyperventilating. Eventually the *Times* article came out – on the front page of the Sunday Arts and Leisure section – and it mentioned my contribution. And as the Larsons came to understand my involvement they agreed to reasonable terms for my "credit and compensation".

As Lisa and I approached the Nederlander Theater for the Broadway opening of *Rent*, film crews shined lights on newscasters who interviewed sparkly celebrities as models and stars walked from shiny limos dressed in glittery stuff that shimmered as cameras flashed. Inside the theater people shimmied through the packed aisles slyly peeking at people who were slyly peeking at them. Lisa and I made our way up to the balcony and took our seats in the second to last row of the theater, high above all the sly peeking. No one in that entire packed theater knew I was there and that was just fine. Feeling pure and clean in my anonymity I could relax and observe the whole event from above.

The actors took the stage, the audience screamed and cheered. The actor playing Mark dedicated "this and every performance of *Rent* to our friend, Jonathan Larson," and looked up at the ceiling. A thousand atheists looked up at the ceiling and cheered and stomped and screamed. As the show began I came to understand the term "show stopper"; after nearly every song, the audience clapped and howled for so long that the actors couldn't just pause, they had to come to a complete stop and stand there waiting. The songs I'd written with Jonathan years ago were still there, though some lyrics had changed along the way. I missed the intimacy of the Off Broadway production, but it seemed to me that the show's big cast, big themes, and big emotions made it work just fine on the big stage. Critics agreed.

When I eventually met Jonathan Larson's father Allan, I told him that his son was like Babe Ruth, who had allegedly pointed to the center field fence before hitting a home run right over it. With Jonathan there was no allegedly. I was there. I sat on that rooftop when he said this show would be our generation's *Hair* and bring young audiences back to the theater. Before a word of the show had been written he announced what he'd do, and in spite of what everyone – myself included – thought possible, through 7 years of hard work for no money, he did it. Critics described *Rent* as a new *Hair* as Jonathan had envisioned from the start. And as *Rent* opened in theaters across the country and around the world, the show did bring a new audience to the theater – a younger, savvy, diverse audience looking for stories about the way we live now expressed through contemporary forms of music. Producers responded by bringing Off Broadway hits like *Fun Home, Next to Normal, Spring Awakening*, and *Dear Evan Hansen* to Broadway.

After its triumphant Broadway opening *Rent* was sold out for months. The cast album came out featuring a bonus track performance with Stevie Wonder. Subway cars were filled with posters of beautiful angry young people wearing the torn black outfits of a new *Rent*-inspired clothing line. Characters in other plays and TV shows (eventually *The Sopranos, Girls, The Office...*) began referencing *Rent*.

As *Rent* moved across the country and then to Europe and Asia it spread hope, inspiration, and joy wherever it went. At the same time it made a lot of my theater friends feel like crap. Artistic directors whose productions were being ignored and composers who dreamed of creating the next big hit confided in me, moaning. There was no way the press could go absolutely insane for a show again for decades. So why go on?

Rent got into my head too. While trying to write my own stuff I'd find my mind crafting long and winding answers to the *Rent*-related questions I'm constantly asked. Eventually I was able to simplify my answers so I could dispense with the questions quickly. For example:

Q: Would you trade places with Jonathan Larson?

A: No.

Q: Do you regret letting Jonathan go ahead with *Rent*?

A: No.

Q: Do you wish you were a Tony-winning Obie-winning Pulitzer-winning multi-millionaire with adoring fans around the world saying you've changed their lives?

A: Yes.

Q: Were you and Jonathan lovers?

A: No.

Q: Did Jonathan die of AIDS?

A: No.

Q: But wasn't *Rent* his "One Song Glory"?

A: No. Though the character Roger yearns to create one great song while dying of AIDS, Jonathan had an undetected heart problem related to his genetic condition called Marfan syndrome. While writing *Rent*, he had no idea his time was short.

Q: Did Jonathan steal your idea?

A: No.

Q: What would your *Rent* be like?

A: I never wrote my *Rent*.

Q: In your *Rent* did Mimi die?

A: I never wrote my *Rent*.

Q: Did you write "Seasons of Love"?

A: No.

Q: Did you write the lyrics for "Seasons of Love"?

A: No.

Q: Was it your idea to have a song about how many minutes there are in a--

A: No.

Q: What songs in *Rent* did you write?

A: I don't write music. I wrote lyrics for "Rent", "Santa Fe", and "I Should Tell You".

Q: Are your lyrics still in the show?

A: In my last call with Jonathan he said the lyrics to "Rent" had become pretty much his, "Santa Fe" was pretty much mine, and "I Should Tell You" was half and half. Having seen the finished product I feel he underestimated my contribution but we never got to have that discussion.

Q: How does it feel when the characters on your favorite TV show start singing a song from *Rent*?

A: Frickin' weird.

Q: What's your favorite part of *Rent*?

A: The reprise of "No Day But Today" at the end when different melodies come together.

Q: If Jonathan had lived would the show have taken off the way it did?

A: I can't answer "what if" questions. Reality is way too bizarre to predict.

Q: How would fame have changed Jonathan Larson if he'd lived?

A: I don't know.

Q: Would he have created one great musical after another?

A: I don't know.

Q: Does it bother you when people don't include you in their story about the creation of *Rent*?

A: Yes.

Q: Do you mind when theaters producing your work make a big deal about your *Rent* credit?

A: Theaters that produce my plays can do anything they want.

Q: Are you sick of talking about *Rent*?

A: For years I was but now I'm fascinated by how it all unfolded.

After *Rent* opened a theater agent and a TV agent wanted to work with me, famous song writers wanted to talk about collaborating on new musicals with me, and acquaintances started inviting Lisa and me to dinner so they could talk about how much they loved *Rent* while playing the *Rent* CD. But soon the agents, songwriters, and acquaintances lost interest and I was free to get back to doing my own thing – boosted by 6 *Rent*-inspired lessons that are great news for all of us making our lives in the arts:

LESSON: Your art can change the world.

The things that come out of your head can have an impact on people all over the planet. The power of art is unlimited.

LESSON: Your art doesn't have to change the world.

Your job as an artist is to do what's you, pure you, get it right, get it out there, and let the world do what it's going to do.

LESSON: You don't need to be famous to be a success.

You don't need to have a series of hits to have a career. You don't need to overhear people talking about your work wherever you go, or to have strangers congratulate you in a restaurant. You need a few people in your field to know you and want to work with you, and family and friends who love you.

LESSON: Though artists are usually paid way too little for our work, occasionally we're paid way too much.

After a week the amount I'd earned from *Rent* was enough to cover all my legal fees. After a month it was enough to buy an elephant.

LESSON: While your work can be ignored, rejected, and panned for stupid arbitrary reasons, success can be ridiculously unpredictable too.

You can't know how your work will be received, which of your works will do best, which of your peers will go furthest, how current events might transform tastes, or what people will think of you when you're dead. All you can do is:

LESSON: Dream, reach, risk, love, and when collaborating get *something in writing.*

CHAPTER 8.
LEARNING FROM THE AUDIENCE

When I arrived in New York in the fall of 1983 one of the first people I contacted for advice was Yale playwright Harry Kondoleon who told me: "All the doors are closed, then all the doors open, then sometimes they close again."

Though Harry had only been in town for 2 years his plays were already being produced all over the place and he had just won an Obie Award. I have no idea how Harry Kondoleon knew about closed doors. I, on the other hand, would spend the rest of my twenties, all of my thirties, and into my forties going door to door, banging on them all, desperate to get someone to do my plays.

LESSON: Infinite passion + infinite patience.

Finally, in the spring of 1998, two doors opened at once. A short play I'd written called "Dream" was chosen for the annual Marathon of One-Act Plays at Ensemble Studio Theatre (EST) on West 52nd Street, and my full-length play *The Art Room* was chosen for the upcoming season at the Woolly Mammoth Theatre in DC. These would not be cold readings, rehearsed readings, semi-staged script-in-hand readings or any other kind of substitute for an actual show, but professional productions with sets, costumes, lights, music, makeup, salaries for everybody, and publicity and critics so my work would be "noticed" by the public; no more trees falling unnoticed in the forest of my head. And there would be two of them, two chances for me to reach the public. When I heard Steve Wonder singing "For Once in My Life" on the radio I felt he was singing about me; I was finally living the life I was meant to live.

The EST Marathon was the only place in town where one-act plays were fully produced every year. With its low-budget productions the festival was both spare and glamorous; dozens of busy professional actors including a movie star or two (Rosie Perez, Kevin Bacon...) would appear on EST's intimate main stage in new short works by famous writers (Arthur Miller, Joyce Carol Oates...) and a few very lucky unknowns. For 15 years I'd been submitting short plays to EST in the fall and having them rejected in the spring. After years of rejection I considered not submitting out of spite, but the dream of having a play in the EST Marathon always won out.

At auditions for my Marathon play I was in playwright heaven, as actors I'd been admiring from afar came in to shake my hand and praise the play and do amazing work with my words. But as we began rehearsals I got a creepy feeling something was off. During previews my fears were confirmed.

LESSON: Readings are better for promoting your work than for learning about it.

"Dream" is about a single mom who can't make sense of adulthood. As she tries to organize her plans for the upcoming busy day she speaks with alliteration and rhythm and rhyme, almost like she's singing. In readings of the play the tongue-twisty language gave viewers something lively to listen to as they imagined the play being performed. But when actual audience members filled the seats they weren't there to imagine a play. They were there to root for someone who's struggling to accomplish something. My character's musical speech didn't help her solve anything, or help the audience relate to her as a single mom. In fact, every extra clever-sounding syllable only distracted from her crisis. Night after night I watched our poor actress struggle to engage the audience as her own words got in the way.

When I looked back at plays by writers whose language inspired me I realized that their music is subtle, teasing; they coax poetry out of everyday speech. In Harold Pinter's seductive "Take a sip, a cool sip, sit on my lap and take a sip" (Ruth in *Homecoming*) and Shakespeare's hissing "haste with such dexterity to incestuous sheets" (Hamlet), the sound and rhythm of the words help the characters make their points with power. Even when Ionesco has characters shout "The Pope elopes, the Pope's got no horoscope," his inane rhymes are used to make a mockery of authority figures, sacred values, and human conversation. In Drama School we'd learned that "language comes from character" and I'd always known that the sounds of a character's words matter. But I didn't understand the danger of overdoing the music until I stood behind a full-house of people who were detached from my play.

The *New York Times* said "Dream" was "silly and pretentious" and I can't say I disagree. But since this was my first public evaluation I was crushed. It felt as though I'd been discovered, all right; the world had discovered that I'm bad.

After "Dream" I went through everything I'd written in search of too-musical language and found other bits of cute language that made characters seem light when they most needed weight.

LESSON: More matter with less art.

Young artists with big ambitions tend go for too many trills, twirls, and frills, showing off what they can do outside the work instead of trusting the work itself. After that first production I was determined that my characters would express themselves as simply and plainly as possible, with rhythm and sound determined by the character's nature instead of the playwright's cleverness. The only time I'd let characters speak with adorned language is when they were being silly and pretentious.

The idea for my next produced play, *The Art Room*, came from a 19th century French farce by Georges Feydeau in which a frenzy of deceptions builds to an exhilarating climax. I love Feydeau's play, but as I read it I found myself imagining a version in which those upper class liars were patients in a mental ward. Pathological liar Jon tries to seduce schizoid actress Maddy with the help of infantile Thomas while hiding from his depressive girlfriend Jackie and Maddy's obsessive compulsive husband Art, as Nurse Norma struggles to keep it together. Like most of my plays this one is full of physical business -- grabbing, dancing, dashing, hugging...

A comedy about people suffering from mental illness is a risky idea, which made it perfect for Howard Shalwitz, founder and fearless leader of the adventurous Woolly Mammoth Theatre in Washington, D.C. When Howard decided to produce *The Art Room* I spent the next several months hoping people would ask what I was doing so I could say: "I've got a play coming up at the Woolly Mammoth." I even loved saying "I've got a play coming up at the Woolly Mammoth" to people who had no idea what I was talking about.

But once again, when my work was put on stage for an audience, I learned painful lessons.

LESSON: Costumes change everything.

In staged readings of *The Art Room* that we'd done at EST the actors wore their every day clothes. Though the dialogue alludes to their hospital pajamas, the actors were dressed the same way audience members were, so the characters seemed like the crazy people we know, love, and are. But when the actors appeared on stage at the Woolly in their hospital pajamas it sunk in: These are hospital patients. They're sick. They're suffering. That's sad.

LESSON: Sets change everything.

To lift the show out of naturalism, my director encouraged the set designer to make the stage feel distorted, off kilter, and odd. The result was a stunning set in which all angles were tilted, everything was off balance and unreal, very trippy. I loved it. Everyone loved it. But it was wrong for the play. The bizarre set turned the mental ward into a warped cartoon nightmare. So while jarring the mental patients with its comic twists, the play was making them seem grotesque with an eerie set. The play was not being fair.

LESSON: An audience is a jury.

Though people can laugh at just about anything with their friends, when they come together to watch a public performance they become part of a jury. If a few people laugh at something but no one else laughs, the laughers feel shame; they deemed the show worthy without consulting with the group. Together the audience members ask themselves: Is this show being fair?

During previews the few HAs we got were small and the silence was enormous. We added a wig, sped things up, replaced an actor, cut some lines...I hoped that somehow the critics of Washington D.C. would see what the play was trying to do and help the audience get it instead of delighting in my failure. They did not. As houses dwindled, the actors fought like hell to make audiences laugh, audiences resisted. Mom, Dad, and Dorothy all came with their spouses so my family could see characters like our beloved Joe degraded and mocked by his big brother with an MFA.

LESSON: When what comes out of your head doesn't represent what's in your head you want to remove your head.

Tim Sanford, now artistic director of Playwrights Horizons, came down to the Woolly to see my first produced full-length play. For years he'd been keeping an eye on my work, and I'd been dreaming he'd do a play of mine in New York, but Tim went home disappointed.

After *The Art Room* I vowed *never again* to write characters who are mentally ill, or sick, infirm, disabled in any way. My writing is naturally comedic, I step back from things, look ironically at situations. You can't look ironically at sick people. Or so I thought. A few years later when *The Art Room* was produced at Wellfleet Harbor Actor's Theater I stayed away dreading further humiliation. But the press loved this production, the run was sold out, my friends who tried to get in were actually turned away. Why did the play go well in one situation and not in the other? Since I didn't see the revival I can only guess. But clearly, I needed to un-learn the lesson about not writing characters with infirmities.

LESSON: Question all lessons.

In the arts, rules are suggestions, explanations are guesses, and knowledge is squishy.

In my next play the mental illness was subtle, the style of the language was subtle, the setting was familiar. *Light Years* takes four college students through four years of school in four parts – one for each college year. I used a jerky, clipped style to capture the way time feels to me, not just in college, but from birth and always: sudden shifts, jarring leaps, imagined progress, you're here you're there you're gone and through it all friendship is hard to maintain but most precious. When nobody rushed to do the play I called the first part a one-act play, submitted it to the EST Marathon, and got my next production.

LESSON: When you can't sell something you've created, consider selling part of it.

My go-to director at EST had been Jamie Richards who's great with comedy, has a super rapport with actors, respects my work, and commits to a project with furious devotion. But since Jamie had directed my unhappy "Dream" I decided to look for a "name" director this time. Besides doing a terrific job because of their name-earning talent, the name director's name would attract extra attention to the show; the press loves naming names, audiences love seeing names.

LESSON: People with names want to work with other people with names, preferably bigger names.

After being politely rejected by name after name I begged Jamie to direct for me again and I'm so glad she said yes. The two of us worked together much better this time.

LESSON: If you stick with a collaborator you can learn together.

Jamie assembled a cast of 4 sparkling actors in their early twenties: Sarah Rose, Anne Marie Nest, Paul Bartholomew, and Ian Reed Kesler. Each of them understood their characters instantly and totally got the play's funny-serious tone. And they played together so well. During rehearsals I'd find myself creeping up to the playing area until Jamie pulled me back; I couldn't get close enough to the dorm room they filled with their adorableness.

It was all going so smoothly. Too smoothly? Where was the hidden flaw that would turn this production into a humiliation like the others? I went through the play line by line in my mind while riding the subway home, washing dishes, lying in bed...The kids could tell I was preoccupied/possessed. When I forced Anna's arms into her coat too quickly she called me a meanie, but Jake corrected her: "Daddy's not mean, he's just sometimes a maniac."

Eventually the maniac found the flaw he was looking for, the play's final line: "My father died." The whole play leading up to that line is giddy, with swift interchanges about love and friendship and identity. "My father died" isn't giddy and swift. It stuck out. Why had I written it? To seem tragic or deep? When I was alone with my computer that line gave me tingles. But now with audiences on the way I despised "My father died."

At the next rehearsal I had the actors do the play without "my father died." But now something was missing. I added a wordless ending with characters bumping around. Not good. I changed the line to "My father's dying." Maybe that would be less striking? When I brought in a panel of experts to watch my obliging cast, people were puzzled by "dying". Someone said how about just "My father died"? So I left the original in as a placeholder that I never got around to replacing.

On opening night of the one-act "Light Years" the audience went HA a lot. They even clapped in the middle. As the lights came down after "My father died" someone gasped. The next morning at 5 AM I heard the tap of the *New York Times* hitting our front door, ran downstairs, scanned the arts section, no review. Relief. I could go ahead with my day like a normal person until the next morning at 5 AM, and the next and the next and the next, until: the review of EST Marathon Evening A. I moved my eyes across the words, something nice about our play, something else nice, big picture of Sarah and Anne Marie, something nice about the cast, the director, the play, and then something about the next one-act in the evening...That's it? I kept scanning. Nowhere in that entire review did it say Billy Aronson is a terrible person.

I called Jamie, waking her: "We got a good review in the *New York Times*." I read her the review. She disagreed with my assessment. "That was a *great* review." I read it again. The critic even liked "My father died". We raved: "You're so great!" "No you're so great!" "We're both so great!" Later that morning my phone rang and rang and the call-waiting beeps beeped as friends I hadn't heard from in years called to congratulate me and people I hardly knew called to talk about themselves. That night at the theater Jamie and the cast and I all shared extra big hugs and yelped as quietly as possible so people from the other shows wouldn't think we cared about reviews.

As the review got audiences charged up, our actors became so relaxed in their characters that they could trust their onstage impulses, find more of those odd-awkwardness-between-humans moments and the show got better with every performance.

LESSON: As performers trust their own imaginations, they bring to life the thing the creator originally imagined.

Watching from the back of the house, I felt like the archeologists in *Jurassic Park* when they see the dinosaurs for the first time. Remember Laura Dern's expression when speechless Sam Neill reaches down to turn her head with his hand? Those characters are dedicated experts who have been certain of the existence of dinosaurs all their professional lives. But when they actually see dinosaurs lumbering around and nibbling from trees, they become unable to move or speak. Though I'd spent a ridiculous amount of time writing and scrutinizing the script and had considered it from every angle, actually seeing it up and running was shocking. A playwright's most intense joy and profound feeling of triumph can be expressed in the simple words "It works".

Viewing our creation with particular interest was Tim Sanford who hadn't given up on me yet. Tim liked what he saw and decided to take another look at the script of the original full-length version of *Light Years*. Would I like to hear his notes? Yes please. He asked about cuts, I cut. He asked if Jamie and our perfect cast could do a reading of the revised script, everybody said yes. After the reading he had suggestions about the staging; we adored them. He had to look at his budget, check in with other playwrights who owed him scripts, but if he had a slot in his 2001-2002 season, rehearsals beginning Sept 18, could that work for us? YES. In early June of 2001 Tim called again. Silence. Then: "Let's do it."

When you fantasize year after year about your absolutely perfect dream happening a lot of great stuff you never expected might happen but never that exact perfect fantasy thing. And yet, some 16 years after Andre Bishop got me dreaming I'd have a production at his famous theater, it was happening.

That summer I didn't walk around, I bounced. Every day I read through the script remembering the laughs and gasps we got during the first part of the play, imagining laughs, tears, and cheering for the rest. Once in August when I read through the script I was horrified to find that nothing dramatic happened in the last part. So I read that section again from a different perspective and it worked fine. But my favorite summer read was the standard Playwrights Horizons contract, which asked me to grant Playwrights Horizons the right to produce the play and to permit it to be extended and/or moved to another theater off or on Broadway.

As my dream summer turned to fall I sent Playwrights Horizons flyers announcing the production to everyone I knew. A week before the first rehearsal I walked 7-year-old Anna to school under a perfectly clear sky (at 9 Jake was already too old to be seen with me in public) and came home to a call from Lisa telling me that a plane had crashed into one of the World Trade Towers. As the news unfolded I brought the kids home from school and kept them away from the TV, where every channel showed bodies falling from skyscrapers. From outside her office at NYU Lisa saw one of the towers collapse, then headed to the nearest functioning subway stop and had an eerily quiet ride home. Over the coming days Lisa and I acted upbeat for the kids, but when writing my weekly letter to Joe I noticed that the words I was writing looked shaky as though written by an old man.

A week after the infamous day I went into Manhattan to start rehearsing *Light Years* and found pictures of missing people taped all over Times Square, along with shrines with flowers and candles honoring lost firemen. There were police helicopters circling overhead and military jets higher up. Mailboxes had been removed from the area so no one could put bombs in them.

Arriving at the rehearsal space, I hugged Jamie, Sarah, Anne Marie, Paul, Ian, and Tim (my stomach was tight, my legs felt shaky) and met the Playwrights Horizons staff, all gracious and supportive, especially company manager Caroline Aquino, a beautifully upbeat problem solver who elevates good nature to an art form. Tim spoke about how glad he was to be working with us "especially at this time", Jamie spoke about how much it meant to be there "especially at this time", and we read-through the script. Then the staff left and Jamie, the cast, and I picked right back up where we'd left off at EST. While beginning to block out the first scene we heard a low-flying plane out the window getting closer. Everybody stopped. Waited. It passed. Back to blocking.

The Sunday night before the second week of rehearsals I went to bed around 11 and woke up a couple hours later with my mind cycling through terrible thoughts: No one will want to live in New York so our house will have no value. No one will come to population centers so there will be no more productions. My family will have no home and nothing to eat. I will have nothing to do for the rest of my life.

When I got out of bed and lay down on the floor my brain kept racing so I got back in bed and tried to lie flat on my back and breathe. I got back on the floor, curled up into a ball, closed my eyes, went back and forth between bed and floor until the sun came up. I called my Dad who said it sounded like I'd had a panic attack and mentioned a pill called Ativan. I begged my doctor to fit me in *today*, headed to NYU Medical thinking please God don't let him tell me to talk about my childhood or get fresh air and exercise or wait and see how I sleep tonight I need something now please give me that pill. Which he did. That night when I woke up at 1 AM with my heart pounding I took the tiny white pill, felt my whole body relax, fell right back to sleep. Ativan may be a dangerous, addictive drug, but taken as needed it can allow you to keep working and learning and cheering on your play.

At the first preview there were soft laughs throughout, but hardly an actual HA. After the third preview a director who'd also seen the play at EST asked me why the first scene wasn't funny any more. I hated his question but knew he wasn't the only one wondering. At EST the boisterous responses had been constant; during a speech of Paul's he got giggles after every line and sometimes applause at the end. But in our new venue those friendly sounds were replaced by horrible silence. We kept working to get back the laughs with the help of Tim who watched and had notes every night. I trimmed the script, Jamie kept drilling the actors, and they kept pushing through the leaping, ducking, dancing, wrestling, sleepwalking...

As the show got tighter and clearer audiences were still quiet. At one preview Jamie and I found ourselves sitting behind three people who couldn't stand the play, right from the beginning. After every few lines they looked at one another in disbelief, mouthing silent exclamations like "What that--?!" and "Can you believe--?!" and ten minutes into the show they got up and left. It had never occurred to me that people could hate my work that much.

Even more disturbing was the gradual realization that I'd done a bad job writing the last part of the play. In readings, Anne Marie and Sarah performed their reconciliation scene so beautifully that their lines about how far they'd come made people cry. But in actual performance audience members wouldn't take the script's word for it that the characters were getting somewhere, they had to see it happen. By the last previews I feared that I'd left out important steps in the drama and was sending our brave young actors on a mission that couldn't be accomplished.

The opening performance was perfect, every moment. The full house of Playwrights people and friends loved it, cheered the actors on the whole time. Tim focused intently on every line and clenched fists "yes!" when the audience laughed. Jamie and I sat in back, cooing and glowing like the world's proudest parents. Afterwards there was a party and when I walked in everyone clapped. When I found myself standing near the champagne table, not drinking, just standing there, I noticed Paul and Anne Marie standing there too. Paul said, "This is a great moment". Ian and Sarah and Jamie joined us and we had our picture taken for *Playbill.*

When it was time to head back to Brooklyn I shared a cab ride with Tim who was quiet. After I thanked him for believing in me all those years Tim said, "I like your writing, Billy. It's 'sui generis'". Thanks to my high school Latin I knew that means "of its own kind". Tim Sanford himself is "sui generis". He says exactly what he means, gives frank and clear feedback with humility, always being careful not to mislead a playwright who might have been hoping for "It's a masterpiece" or "I can't wait to do your next play". When I brought up the subject of reviews Tim went into a tirade. "Why should they notice your play, Billy?" He pointed out the window. "It's like the critics are driving past all those stores without stopping or even slowing down. Why should they stop and notice yours?" He continued, "When the critics get a play of ours, I want to say how come you didn't get this other one, or this one, or any of these?" I had never considered that artistic directors could have their hearts broken just like playwrights. Looking back, I suppose Tim had already seen our *Times* review.

When I heard the newspaper hit the door the next morning I kept my eyes closed. Lisa slipped out of bed and hurried downstairs. I heard the front door open and shut. A minute passed. I could not stand the silence. A strong *Times* review would mean our play would be extended, maybe move to a bigger theater, maybe be produced all across the country, my career would take off. I went down to find Lisa at the table with her back to me. "Is it in there?" She nodded. "He didn't get your play." No take off. I glanced at the review to see what I could see. The review wasn't mean. It was "meh". I realize critics are intelligent viewers who see lots of theater and that their frank comments can be valuable. But I had no interest in watching my dear struggling child through the eyes of a critic, and could never bring myself to read that review.

When Tim called to see how I was doing he pointed out that the *Times* said part of the play was "funny" and "smart", so the Playwrights Horizons publicity team could use those words for advertisements. Critics don't have to give you such reprintable gifts; Michael Feingold once referred to a play of mine as having "neat twists" and "good yucks", phrases you'll never see on the side of a bus. Though I managed to avoid the dozens of papers, magazines, and online publications that covered the play, I could tell from Tim's general comments that none of the critics liked (or "got", as we prefer to say) my play. One review made Tim so mad he sent the critic a book on modern drama.

Back at the theater I put on my happy face for the cast and they put on happy faces for me. I watched nearly all of the remaining performances – from backstage, that cozy womb of darkness where techies in black arrange set pieces and props, and actors catch their breath, stand focused, then head back out into the light. I was focused too. Perched on a crate, I listened to every word the actors spoke and every sound the audience made in response. On a good day there was a rhythmic relationship between actors and audience that I could dance to. A first scene speech of Ian's that had a series of BLAHs got laughs every night, but a couple times the BLAHs got nothing and I knew we were in for an uphill battle. Because the main set was removed after the first two parts of the play, during last part I could peek around the backdrop to observe the dozen or so audience members who were illuminated by light from the stage. I could tell when they were into what they were watching, when they were expecting something, and when they were disappointed, line by line, beat by beat. When my Mom and Dorothy came their infectious guffaws inspired one of our best shows. But there continued to be people who couldn't sit through the whole 80 minutes. I could tell when there were walk-outs because the actors came off stage looking crushed.

After the show I would leave my safe zone to greet people I'd invited. Many either avoided talking about the play or pretended not to see me as they headed for the door. A brave few managed to say polite things about the play. In polite-ese "wonderful" means "terrible". "So much fun", "we loved it", and most other vaguely cheerful responses are also polite translations.

So how can you tell if someone actually means what they're saying?

LESSON: It's easy to tell if someone genuinely loves your work.

When you see something that rocks your world you come again, you bring friends, you ask where you can get the script/score/recording, you explain your feelings to the creator in detail with specific references to the work while staring into their eyes. I love people who get excited about my work, but I love the friends who respond politely just as much for having the courage and imagination to find something kind to say.

LESSON FOR FRIENDS OF ARTISTS: When our work isn't good we know. What we don't know is if we deserve to live.

On the night of the last performance we were hoping for a big noisy audience but wound up with a small quiet one, which I blame on Game 7 of the World Series. As I watched the actors do their preshow warm ups and take their places one last time it seemed unfair that our play had to end just because we were the only ones who loved it. After the show, Jamie and I took the cast out to a bar where the TV showed a pair of absurd non-hits end the Yankees' three year reign as World Champions. It was a cold Sunday night in November. It was late. We said goodbye to one another and went our separate ways in a world that had never heard of our play.

"We learn through suffering," I was taught in a college course on tragedy. I learned so much from *Light Years*.

LESSON: Problems don't go away.

When I read the last section of the script in August and thought it had problems, I was right. I'm not sure I could have done a better job at the time; that part needed to be about approaching the end of life, and I was still figuring out my middle. I wish I'd considered doing a rewrite, but with production looming I was too scared to acknowledge the problem. When I got notes from Tim questioning a line, speech, or scene, I had zero confidence in my ability to come up with something better so I just cut the line, speech, or scene. I wish I'd considered rewriting to make the questionable stuff work instead of losing it, but with production looming I was scared.

And what about that horrible shift in audience response when we moved the play 9 blocks from EST to Playwrights Horizons? Among the reasons I considered are:

1. More intimate space at EST.

2. Greater expectations at Playwrights.

3. Osama Bin Laden.

After obsessively trying to figure out what went wrong I gave up and focused on other things -- like listening to my wife and children when they're talking to me.

LESSON: Fail with pride.

People celebrate graduate degrees and mourn failed productions. For me, it should be the other way around. From observing the audiences at *Light Years*, I got a clear sense of how people respond and don't respond to my writing. I learned so much from my failure that I stopped failing. Every play of mine that got produced after *Light Years* pleased a majority of audiences, impressed most critics, and allowed me to see my dinosaur. Having learned to express myself in scripts that could work on stage, I emerged from the experience with a 10 step process that has served me ever since:

1. Start with an idea you love. (Not like. Not admire. Love.)

If you're going to spend many months alone at a computer for hardly any dollars that thing you're typing better turn you on and give you chills and make you giggle and weep.

2. Write.

The first scene is the hardest, the first line nearly impossible, so be patient. Make an outline so you have a sense where you're heading, but keep changing it as the writing takes off. It's easier to solve writing problems while running, doing dishes, anything but staring at a screen, so allow yourself many breaks. Avoid getting input while you're writing; no one can tell what you're doing until you've done it.

3. Revise.

Rewrite to make the play more bold and clear but not tidy. Tidy is the enemy of art. Better to write a section over again from scratch to retain freshness than trim and snip. While loving the project, be your own toughest critic. If you sense there might be a problem, there is. So stop and fix it. (As opposed to having a reading to see if anybody notices.) Ask yourself: Is this thing giving you chills? Are you loving every line? Is the script going as far as it possibly can to get the inspiration you started with out there in a way that every single person will feel? Don't let the script out of the house until you've gotten it right.

4. Find people to do the play.

Make contact with producers directly, without an agent if possible, so producers feel your love and you feel their feelings. The production can be low budget or no budget as long as it's *real*, not hypothetical.

5. Choose a director.

The ideal director is someone who's loved by actors, shares your taste, and gets your work, but what matters most is having someone you can really talk to. (Step 5 can happen before 4, since directors often have connections to theaters.) When you get the production:

6. Listen to your collaborators.

Comments from actors are the best notes you'll ever get; these people have to make your play work in front of an audience so their questions are practical and crucial. Before a reading of the *Light Years*, Anne Marie asked what the conflict was in the last section. If only I'd taken her question as a clue that something was wrong instead of explaining away her concern. Pay attention to feedback from the director too, and producers, designers, dramaturg, stage managers - anyone whose name will be on the program. They want this play to work as much as you do.

7. Guard the script.

Consider all suggestions and notes. But the script is the author's ultimate responsibility. Resist making suggested changes just to seem like a team player. Defending the script is your unique role on the team, so don't be afraid of seeming defensive.

8. Listen to the audience.

It's easy to tell if someone's lusting for the person they're dancing with, rooting for a player in a tennis match, or enjoying your play. As you observe the people observing your play, their posture, breathing, giggles, and grunts tell you all you need to know.

9. Whatever happens, take a victory lap.

Creating something you love and putting it out into the world is an act of bravery and generosity. Regardless of the response, you deserve to feel proud. So celebrate.

10. Start the next one. *Now.*

After *Light Years* I tried to start a new play but self-doubt made it hard to get far. As I wrote I kept seeing those three people in front of me who had been disgusted by every word they heard. I tried to block them out. They kept coming back. Finally I took them on. When they appeared I'd say "Okay bitches let's do this thing," and go deeper into the characters I was writing, make the conflict more vicious, the love more vivid, the relevance so palpable that the Three Evil People would have to feel something and stop on their way out the door and Get the Fuck Back in Their Seats. That got things flowing. And it felt so great to be working again.

LESSON: They can pan you, mock you, ignore you, but they can't stop you.

※ ※ ※

CHAPTER 9.

LEARNING TO CHANGE YOUR EXPECTATIONS

When I sent my next play after *Light Years* to my favorite theaters the doors were closed. Encouraging maybes and offers for readings that I used to get after 1-2 months were replaced by form letter rejections after 6 months. My decades-long plan of marching through Playwrights Horizons to a fancy career was over.

I walked with a slouch, avoided eye contact, and frowned in photos for a few months. But while brooding I kept submitting one-acts to EST and they kept being selected for the Marathon. So I pulled an ugly duckling, decided I wasn't an ugly writer of full-length plays after all but a beautiful writer of one-acts.

LESSON: To succeed in the arts, define what you're doing as success.

Adjusting to swan mentality, I realized that EST offered the greatest gift any playwright could have: a company of actors dedicated to doing your work year after year. My steady director Jamie Richards cast my marathon plays from a pool of actors who were familiar with my style, so nobody balked when asked to start chanting into their cell phone or making conversation with a giraffe. Through these productions (there were 8 altogether) I was able to put my pet obsessions on stage in the funny/

serious tone that turns me on, express my love and my lust, do something with the odd logic of my childhood, point out things that confused me and cracked me up, confront my fear of losing my sanity and my guilt at having it, call out to people who left me and thank friends for sticking around.

LESSON: Some heads just get your head.

The actor we used most in the marathon plays was Thomas Lyons McHugh. Tom is great at combining offbeat humor with heart and could have played any role in any play of mine. In one of my Marathon plays Tom went back and forth between playing a twisted warlock and a hapless lonely guy, stealing the show as each character. Another MVP was our go-to leading lady Geneva Carr. Something from the darkness of Geneva's childhood allowed her to express the darkness in mine. As I watched her bring my characters to life I couldn't believe there was so much anger in them, or her, or me. Director Jamie Richards was an absolute master at making plays work on a miniscule budget, within the world's tightest schedule, on that small stage where our ensemble within the Ensemble coalesced every spring. Though our plays shared a bill with others and only ran for a few weeks, afterwards we'd go out for drinks feeling like theater royalty.

No one becomes a playwright to write short plays. They don't move to big theaters or win Pulitzers. But as I allowed myself to inhabit the pond in which I found myself, I came to see short plays as a perfect form of expression for me. While I enjoy a good 3-act story or seeing a meaty role performed by a star, those full-length-friendly things aren't what brings me to theater. I come to the theater to see our lives for the first time. That doesn't have to take two hours. Instead of reading and re-reading the towering masterpieces of Shakespeare, Chekov, and Ibsen when in the library or on the subway, I started worshipping a different set of iconic works:

*"Not I" by Samuel Beckett

No one has captured the strangeness of living with a brain inside your skull as well as Beckett does in this 15-minute drama carried by a single mouth chattering away like mad as it floats in the darkness.

*"Drowning" by Irene Fornez

In this 10-minute play Fornez makes me feel the same kind of big love for her 3 pathetic potato-shaped beings that I feel for Chekov's 3 sisters. They're me right now. They're all of us always.

*"The Dutchman" by Amiri Baraka

Baraka's play sums up American politics, culture, and history without pomp or pretense in a single act using only 2 characters -- a black man sitting on a subway and a white woman who flirts with him and then destroys him.

*"The Bald Soprano" by Eugene Ionesco

Ionesco's "anti-play" about 2 British couples having an after-dinner conversation is so revolutionary that it started a movement (Theater of the Absurd) and so entertaining that it holds the world record for longest running show (70 years and counting, in Paris).

Compressed masterpieces like these are not "just" one-acts.

LESSON: Short can be full.

When other playwrights talk about the different ways you should approach writing a one-act and a full-length I have no idea what they're talking about. The only difference between a short play and a long play is length. That's it. Because a short play will probably share an evening and a modest budget with other plays, in writing the short play you should use as few characters as possible and not depend on a big set or expensive props. But you should do those things anyway. I assume a small budget for all my plays and keep things minimal regardless of length. With every play I take the initial inspiration as far as it can possibly go, pushing to extremes as aggressively as I would if writing Wagner's 18 hour *Ring* Cycle (which dramatizes the rise and fall of the entire universe). Then I compress, force myself to get right to the point with every scene, speech, and line. How can I ask people to sit still for a single word that isn't crucial? As my Wagnerian conception is slashed to its bare essentials the result tends to be a one-act play.

LESSON: In the arts, size doesn't matter.

Modern dance pieces that make up only part of an evening have blown me away (Alvin Ailey's "Revelations" is 30 minutes, David Parsons' "Caught" is 5) in a way full-length ballets never have. Short stories have made as great an impact as novels, plus I can read them in a sitting instead of over the course of a summer. Songs have been a much bigger part of my life than symphonies. Yes the vast ceiling of the Sistine Chapel is unforgettable but so is the Mona Lisa's 3-inch smile.

Thinking of my one-acts as songs, dance pieces, or compressed full-lengths in the tradition of Beckett, Fornez, and Baraka allowed me to feel proud of what I was doing and inspired to keep doing it.

❋ ❋ ❋

CHAPTER 10:
LEARNING TO STAND BEING OUT THERE

We who make our lives in the arts tend to be 1) quite comfortable being in our heads with our thoughts, and 2) obsessed with expressing what's inside us to the outside world. But while the inside feels safe and cozy, the outside is unpredictable and out of control. Even my bravest performer friends get the jitters before going out there.

If there's a "duck and cover" gene, I have it. Maybe it was a favorable variation from the centuries of pogroms and persecution; if you showed your head, you lost it. When I was 3 my favorite thing to do was lie on the living room couch watching the dust specks float in the sunlight. I had no interest in going to a birthday party where there'd be lots of kids I didn't know, and was even ambivalent about my own birthday party; when the other kids sang happy birthday to me I had to look away.

As my plays started getting done regularly in the early 2000's, anxiety came and stayed. From the moment I learned a play of mine had been chosen for production I'd have serious doubts about the script. The negative thinking would last through rehearsals and become full-blown dread in time for opening night. At first I accepted that I was The Tortured Artist, we suffer for our art, fine. But people would say why can't you just sit in the audience with us and feel proud and happy about how well this is going? Those people had a point.

LESSON: Artists have a right to enjoy our lives.
Our work may be constant struggle, but it's the struggle we chose, fought for, and waited in line for the chance to endure. So we need to stop slinking around and smile.

When anticipation of a particular review made my head an unbearable place to be I decided to let someone else in there, and found a therapist. Taking a seat on the therapist's couch I was struck by the silence. I tried to get him to talk about his work, that wasn't happening. No small talk at all. The spotlight was on me.

"So why are you here?" he asked.

"I'm ashamed of myself," I said. The words surprised me.

"Why are you ashamed of yourself, Billy?"

I tried to say "I don't know" but couldn't because I'd begun bawling. I remember feeling all that warm moisture coming down across my face and hearing the sound of myself sobbing, marveling at the way the sobbing just kept going, feeling embarrassed to be crying in the company of another adult and wondering what I would say when it stopped. Many Kleenexes later I was able to talk about my parents' divorce and my brother's mental illness, and fill my therapist in about my wife and kids and work. He said it was puzzling that I felt ashamed since I was so successful in every aspect of my life. I had no idea what he was talking about.

In weekly meetings my therapist helped with my self-loathing, and that terrible habit of constantly imagining the worst possible outcome. Why the negative brain? We never figured that out, but agreed that I had to stop constantly anticipating disaster. There was no quick fix, but when I could catch myself imagining the worst and imagine better, I was able to look forward to rehearsals in the morning and happy-think myself back to sleep at night.

In the spring of 2009 my ability to enjoy my life was put to the test when I found myself with 4 upcoming productions: My new full-length *First Day of School* was going to have simultaneous premieres on the east and west coasts, my Marathon play "Little Duck" was opening before those, and even sooner a children's musical *Click Clack Moo* for which I'd written the book would premiere Off Broadway. All these openings were a playwright's dream, a stream of blessings. Over the next 5 months I had to keep reminding myself that.

LESSON: As book writer for a musical, you lay the foundation upon which everyone else stomps. I mean builds.

Did you know that the *Sound of Music* is by Rogers and Hammerstein -- and Lindsay and Crouse? Everybody goes wild for the songs in their favorite musicals, but nobody cares who took responsibility for figuring out the story and establishing the characters and writing the dialogue that binds it all together. And that's fine with me. As book writer for a musical you get to be the basketball player who assists, making passes that set up the songwriters for the score that wows the crowd. And if the ball misses the basket, nobody will point at you and boo. So I was delighted when Barbara Pasternak of Theatreworks USA invited me to write the book for a children's musical based on *Click Clack Moo*, a political picture book about cows who learn to stick up for their rights.

But while the audience may not give the book writer much attention, his collaborators do, right from the start. Composer, lyricist, and director all have specific ideas for how the story can set up their work, and the producer has plenty of ideas too. As the New York opening of *Click Clack Moo* approached I was getting sets of notes from four different people on problems I thought we'd solved long ago; sometimes the notes contradicted each other. I wanted to please everybody but kept getting more notes whatever I did, couldn't positive-think my way out of distress, found myself needing Ativan when I woke up in the middle of the night, at afternoon rehearsals where I stuttered like an imposter, and in the evening when I would confront my email to find still more lists of notes. Ativan becomes less effective when used a lot so I felt trapped and scared that I was letting everyone down, the producers, my collaborators, all those kids, I couldn't get that out of my head, wanted to rip the whole thing off my neck. Finally I told Barbara I quit. Let me out. I can't do this. I know how I like things done but if I can't do it my way just tell me what you want and I'll do it your way but when nobody agrees what I should do how can I know what to do?

LESSON: Your collaborators can save you.

Lyricist Kevin Del Aguila is a playwright (and actor) who could have easily finished the book himself and taken my share of the royalties too. I begged him to. But he and composer Brad Alexander wouldn't let me quit. My golden co-authors worked with me to make sense of the notes and figure out how to solve the remaining story problems, saving the day, and my royalties. Our singing cows got their blankets from the farmer and kids from all over town cheered.

Next up was my marathon play "Little Duck", a satirical farce about sadomasochism at a children's TV company. Rehearsals were going fine, but as opening night approached I convinced myself that my parade of theatrical perversion would be a stinky disaster. Unable to sleep through the night with the help of Ativan, I went to the drug store and found a sleep medicine but decided not to take it because it "may tend to be habit forming" (addiction scares me almost as much as bad reviews), went to an herbal back-to-nature type store, was introduced to all different plant-based sleep medicines which again "may tend to be habit forming" so I kept waking up at 3 AM and lying there. My therapist said don't just lie there, get up and read with low lights or listen to music for an hour then go back to bed for a half hour, if you're still awake get back up, etc. During my sitting up stints I recited a series of prayers a friend had sent me; they helped me focus and relax. Also calming were meditation CDs from another friend; I'd sit in the dark listening to Jack Kornfield's gentle voice describing the wisdom of the Buddha. But still I kept waking up in the middle of the night with a head full of awful thoughts and feeling crappy in the morning.

Finally my therapist said it was time to see a psychiatrist who might prescribe an SSRI – a type of anti-depressant that also works for anxiety and can be taken for years without losing its power.

LESSON: Don't choose a psychiatrist based only on location.

In desperation I dashed to a psychiatrist 3 blocks away who told me he didn't believe in SSRIs, they're placebos that make drug companies rich, and suggested I try religion. An orthodox Jew himself, he said I shouldn't bother with the "soft stuff" but should commit to a religious practice that was "serious and strong". I told him that I love religion but don't happen to believe in one. So he wrote me a prescription for Klonopin, Ativan's cousin, and said it might help if I alternated between the two. It didn't.

LESSON: Some psychiatrists offer pills but not compassion.

Next I secured an appointment with one of the few psychiatrists in Brooklyn who accepts health insurance; it was a long wait to get an appointment and when I got there his waiting room was packed. A few sentences into my sob story he cut me off and said I should take the SSRI Lexipro every night for the rest of my life. Taken aback by his swift conclusion I insisted I was going through a tough period but didn't need to be constantly medicated.

"Everybody says that," he answered. "You have social anxiety, general anxiety, some obsessive compulsion, and chronic dysthymic depression."

"I'm a playwright!" I said. "We're all like that!"

While rejecting his blunt diagnosis I took one Lexipro that night, one the next night, and then threw the pills away. For over 50 years my head had been the place to which I could retreat for control, the last bastion of me. No way was I giving up control of my head to chemicals.

Whatever I was suffering from, the quickest fix was a good review. When Jamie reached my cell to quote a critic's description of "Little Duck" as "the Marx Brothers without censorship" I had a blissful walk home and felt buzzed through the run of the show.

LESSON: You shouldn't need a good review to make you feel like a good person.

But I did. The high I got from official approval lifted all bad thoughts and angst, until it was time for the simultaneous premieres.

I wrote *First Day of School* as a prank against adulthood, like I was ramming a stick into the spokes to watch my whole grown-up world go flying. The play features a group of married parents who drop off their kids at kindergarten and find themselves wanting to touch the naked bodies of other married parents. People found *First Day* more accessible than my other work but my wife did not enjoy them having that access. After hearing a reading of the play she told me that my satirical take on monogamy made her feel hurt and embarrassed.

LESSON: Embarrassing your loved ones sucks.

When I write a play I can disguise the specifics about people and places that inspired me but my general feelings still come out. I wish my inner impulses were all noble. Or at least cool. Sometimes they're icky. But when you commit to a life of making art you can't choose how much of what's inside you to use and how much to hide to avoid embarrassing people, your only choice is to give it everything you've got or find another life.

After being presented in countless readings, *First Day of School* was picked up for production by two adventurous regional theaters at a terrible time for adventurous regional theaters. During the financial crisis of 2007-9 the economy of the entire planet nearly fell apart so everybody who had dollars was clinging to them for dear life. Bill English and Susi Damilano, the unstoppable couple at the helm of the San Francisco Playhouse, managed to get donors to donate and subscribers to subscribe while helping the show go on by rolling up their sleeves and coaching, acting, designing, and baking. Meanwhile at Philadelphia's all comedy theater 1812 Productions, the 5 actors playing parents struggling to pay the bills while raising young kids were all in fact parents struggling to pay the bills while raising young kids. One of those multi-tasking stars, Jennifer Childs, was also running the theater.

Actors in each cast had moments of panic during rehearsals, producers got nervous and asked for last minute cuts, but I was generally able to hold my ground and reassure people things would be okay. Overall everybody in both productions was able to focus and commit to the work. I saved my Ativan for the daily rehearsal/run-thru/preview, avoided negative thinking the rest of the day by taking long runs and doing pushups, and was able to enjoy watching two strong productions of my work come to life.

As the show opened on both coasts I found myself with an unexpected third gift: a controlled experiment in which I could compare productions to learn about my work with a precision that was almost scientific.

LESSON: For physical business, house size matters.

In *First Day* there's a 3-character wrestling match/orgy on a couch, narrated by a fourth character. Both productions of the play worked hard to choreograph this scene and made it work. But in the intimate black box theater at the SF Playhouse where everybody in the house was within a few yards of the stage, people in the audience could see the actors' facial expressions, the movements of their hands, the shifting of their weight, and feel caught up in their situation. In the standard proscenium stage in Philly where nobody was that close to the stage (many were in the balcony), people chuckled appropriately, but weren't breathing and squirming in their seats along with the action as they were in San Francisco.

While distance between actors and audience mattered for the physical business, it didn't seem to make any difference for the dialogue and monologues. Always audible, the actors in both productions got audience responses in the same places.

LESSON: For laughter, house size matters.

Though the productions got laughs in the same parts of the play, the production in the bigger theater got bigger laughs. And I couldn't believe how great that felt. With our marathon plays in EST's black box space, sometimes an audience of up to 75 people would laugh right from the beginning of a play, but sometimes they'd sit there quietly waiting for one laugher to give everybody else permission to go HA. In 1812's theater that seats 300 there were always plenty of people laughing right from the beginning. The laughter would build and move through the house, from orchestra to balcony and back, becoming like a character itself. As a member of the audience at a comedy, I can have a fine time if no one's laughing. But what a treat it is to share spontaneous outbursts with hundreds of strangers, as you join everyone in the house and on the stage in a cathartic conversation ("You're human!" "I'm human!" "We're all human!") And as an author, to have hundreds of people all around you and above just letting go and laughing out loud at your words at the same moment is an indescribable high.

LESSON: Comedy is funny.

After performances at 1812, comedy fans would ask me how to be funny. I wanted to reveal a secret strategy but had to be honest: I'm not aware of following any particular rule to get laughs. In fact, things that shouldn't be funny can make people laugh the most. There's something illogical about the whole business.

There are standard tricks like the rule of 3 -- If something happens three times, the first two can set up a pattern that the third can break to get a laugh. Also: if there are two people who shouldn't meet under any circumstances, have them meet as soon as possible. Flying food is good, and weak people toppling powerful people, grownups falling down, sudden surprises, puns, clowns...But those things don't always lead to laughs. Shakespeare uses the rule of 3 in his darkest tragedy *King Lear*, as Lear's first two verbose daughters provide the perfect set up for the third daughter to say nothing, but nothing funny comes of her nothing. *Lear* also has the world's least funny flying food, the infamous "vile jelly" that comprises an old man's eyes, as well as puns aplenty – all suggesting that the world's about to end, Shakespeare's most depressing clown – an existentialist fool who should never do birthday parties, powerful old men brought down by sadistic youngsters, sudden surprises intended to bring joy that cause heart attacks, and a dramatic climax in which all the characters who should never meet do meet until everyone's dead.

Left without a single rule for making people laugh, I'm aware of a few things I do that sometimes make/coax/allow people to go HA:

*Cut to the bone. Not a wasted word.

*Pay attention to rhythm, of both language and action. Speed can be good. But so can slowing down, even coming to a sudden halt. Comedy captures the jerky rhythm of our lives.

*Think visually, especially in terms of what bodies are doing to each other. Human bodies kicking, pushing, tripping, sucking, pouncing, licking, and grabbing can cause human bodies watching to guffaw.

*Give the audience a sense of what's up, but don't nail it down with too many details. Nervous uncertainty makes me giggle.

*Steal from funny sources. I've drawn comedic situations from Chaucer's Canterbury Tales, the Winnebago trickster myths, the comedies of Plautus, Shakespeare, and Moliere, and the cartoons of Bunny (Bugs).

*Present life's horrors with perspective. Shakespeare's dark picture of human beings as animals ruled by their genitals becomes a scream when framed by fairies in *A Midsummer Night's Dream*. *Put your whole oddball self out there. In daily life you get so many signals that you should hide your weirdness, censor your thoughts, disguise your smell, anything to avoid sticking out. Funny sticks out.

The most important thing I learned, conclusively, from my parallel productions:

LESSON: A bad review doesn't mean you suck.

Everyone knows that. Nobody believes it. We secretly believe that the theater critic from the biggest paper in town knows and tells the truth. It's a news paper, after all. It reports the facts. But after the critic from the *San Francisco Examiner* wrote a lovely review of *First Day* that led to more productions in the west and a Bay Area Theater Award for best new play, the reviewer from *The Philadelphia Inquirer* responded to the same script (not the production, which she found flawless) with unmitigated loathing. By flatly contradicting the SF review, the Philly critic shoved my face up against a hard fact: I have to decide for myself if I'm any good.

The San Francisco cast received a nomination for Best Ensemble Performance and should have gotten one for Best Marijuana at an Opening Night Party; after I toasted everybody for their great work in hard times we had a celebration so memorable that I can't remember it. Every night of the Philly production was a celebration with members of my extended family and friends from my youth who came to see the show and go HA. Lisa made it to that production and loved it (I do love her), and at the final performance I was as proud of the play as I was of the talented high school actress sitting next to me, my little girl Anna.

And then it was over.

LESSON: Sleep comes back.

After four months of waking up in the dark and wondering what to do with myself, I had come to believe I'd never sleep through the night again. But in the rush of endorphins that followed my quadruple deliveries, I could once again go to bed at night and sleep until morning. I was able to get off the anxiety pills too. The angst was all gone.

With my head clear, I finished a pair of one-acts in time for publication in a collection of my short plays called *Funny Shorts*. Though the cover photo of me in my underwear (both photo and underwear selected by my marketing-savvy son Jake) reveals my copious fur and folds I don't feel embarrassed by it at all, probably because when the plays inside the book were produced it felt like I was standing completely naked in a spotlight as strangers inspected me from close enough to smell my sweat. Compared to the experience of having a play produced, being nearly naked on a book cover is no problem.

After I die I'd like to watch my life play out all over again so I can figure out what was actually going on the whole time. In the meantime, among the few things I'm sure of are that I was born, I will die, and for most of the years in between playwriting has been my way of life. Through the efforts of actors on a stage I've been able to share my life with audiences of people who've given me the supreme honor of paying attention. There's been some cheering, but mostly I remember all the cheering up and cheering on, everybody rooting for each other, producers and directors rooting for the audience to root for the characters as I was rooting for the actors from my corner of the darkness, and somewhere else in that same darkness my loved ones were rooting for me. And what friends I made along the way – not in spite of the tension but because of it. I fell in love with every one of those casts. We shared the fear and thrills for a short time, then everybody let go and moved on. But whenever I run into someone from one of my shows, whether after 4 years or 40, we share warm memories of the work we did together.

LESSON: Putting yourself out there is always hard but always worth it.

After the last performance of my first college play I sat on stage with the actors, pretending to drink a beer as we talked about plays, finals, parents…It was the first college party I actually enjoyed. Around midnight I headed back to my room somehow managing to carry piles of salvaged scripts and programs, the full-sized manikin we'd used as a prop, a pair of plastic buckets, and a bag with the unused balloons. My feet were frozen because I was wearing my sneakers in the snow, being too cool to wear galoshes. I'd gone through my meager savings buying gifts for the actors who had memorized my lines during exam period, so there would be many extra dishwashing shifts in my future. My grades had suffered that semester, I had no girlfriend, I still had a large stretchy face with pimples, I still felt alone in the company of others, and my parents still despised each other, but in the moment that stuff didn't matter so much because I felt as though I was on to something important.

LESSON: *Viva la vie Boheme.*

❋ ❋ ❋

CHAPTER 11:
LEARNING TO BE REBORN

Leaping new hurtles with your art is exhilarating, and necessary. You need to keep setting new challenges, pushing harder and further, finding ways to surprise yourself so you can surprise your audience. Sometimes over a long career you find that there's nowhere left to leap. You're rearranging but not really changing, on the verge of being predictable and boring. So you stop doing this thing that's your way of life. Then what?

After *First Day of School* I was tired of the stuff that was coming out of my head when I sat down to write a play. I'd gone as far as I could with the themes that inspired me and had no more stories that I was dying to tell so I stopped writing plays, moved my *Rent* credit to the top of my resume, and tried to reinvent myself as a creator of musicals. I love being anywhere near music, and was anxious to get somebody else's head together with mine to form a new head with new stuff coming out of it. Thanks to the timing – the *Rent* movie was coming out and the buzz was back, I was able to meet with some of my favorite singer-songwriters and up-and-coming theater composers to talk about projects. In nearly all cases we found that we shared values and passions so we jammed on ideas until we had one we loved, started working together, and then, inevitably, I quit. It never seemed to feel quite right.

LESSON: Sometimes you reinvent yourself, sometimes opportunities reinvent you.

In the spring of 2010 I got a call from Jennifer Oxley, an artist/director of animation I met while head writing a Nickelodeon cartoon called *The Wonder Pets.* I hadn't gotten to know Jen well at the time, mainly because I'd stayed in my closet-sized office all day and dashed for the elevator at quitting time, but I could tell she was hard-working and kind and unusually talented. The visual worlds Jen creates are inventive and brave, more like what you'd find in cool picture books than on kids TV.

Jen was calling to let me know that PBS was looking for a math show for 3-5 year olds, did I want to team up to pitch something? At the time I hated:

1. Television. Watched it of course, but greatly preferred plays/concerts/anything shared with a community of live people.

2. Working in television. Producers gave stupid notes, made me take away the most interesting stuff, cared more about money than quality.

And I especially despised:

3. Children's television. The forced enthusiasm, fake smiles, stupid music. Some kids' shows are all about selling toys. The others -- they call themselves educational -- are weighed down with dull, preachy content. If we want kids to learn about the world, let them go outside and watch birds picking through garbage. Even leaving kids to sit in silence with nothing to do but daydream would be better than helping them develop an addiction to the screen.

In spite of my mixed feelings about TV, with my 18 and 16-year-olds setting their sights on the most expensive universities in all the land, the possibility of a steady income sounded delightful. Plus I was ready for a new adventure. So I said yes to Jen's invitation and discovered that:

LESSON: If you're willing to let go of the rules, assumptions, and habits that have defined your artistic career, you can be reborn into a new one.

Jen and I put our heads together and came up with *Peg + Cat*, a show about a girl and her cat who live inside math word problems that they solve by working together like a left brain/right brain pair: Peg leads the way boldly forward, Cat falls down in useful ways. After all my struggles with collaboration, working with Jen was easy as pie. I never would have believed it but:

LESSON: One character can come from two people.

*A scrappy tomboy who draws wherever she goes, Peg is a lot like Jen; as someone who responds to certain stressful situations by "totally freaking out", Peg has a lot in common with me. *While Cat's design was inspired by Jen's beloved cat Sydney whose amorphous shape fascinated Jen, the way Cat brings about breakthroughs through impulse and accident is a long-time fascination of mine.

Above all, Peg and Cat were meant to be great friends who complement each other perfectly, and as Jen and I worked together that's what we became.

LESSON: A pitch document shouldn't just tell about the project, it should show it.

In our 8 page pitch document I had Peg give the reader a tour of her world in her own chatty, quirky style. I was so proud of the text I wrote -- until I saw it surrounded by Jen's colorful hand drawings of Peg and Cat romping through a world that looked like math: hills, seas, and trees made of simple geometric shapes and clouds shaped like infinity signs, with equations (3+1=4) for the document's page numbers. My instant reaction to Jen's work was: She kicked my ass. She's winning. Then I took a deep breath, and came to see that:

LESSON: In collaboration you don't beat each other, you challenge each other to go further.

We wanted our pitch document to give readers the friendly feeling about math we had in mind for the show, and our readers at PBS got the friendly feeling. They moved us to the next round of their *American-Idol*-like competition, reducing the field from 3 dozen show creators to a final few who would turn their short pitch documents into 50 page show bibles.

The next thing I was surprised to learn is that:

LESSON: Network notes can be helpful.

People with the power to say Do This Or You Have No Show make me nervous. But while I anticipated notes from those people with dread and read them with scorn, Jen saw them as an opportunity to make the show better. When we got notes from PBS, Jen would wait patiently through my whining then point out ways we could respond in a way that would please everybody. Even me.

The only note that bugged us both was a question from PBS about Peg's totally freaking out; doesn't it reinforce the stereotype that girls are scared of math? Over my years in kids TV, every time I had tried to make a girl character funny a well-meaning educational consultant would tell me to make the character less extreme to avoid reinforcing a negative stereotype about girls. While boy characters could be dirty, selfish, pushy, foolish, or obsessed with stuffing cookies in their faces, when it came to girl characters: no funny foibles allowed. A character of any gender has to be extremely *something* to be funny; moderation is boring. And in our particular case with Peg, humans really do freak out about math. How can kids relate to a character who isn't human?

LESSON: It is possible to question a network note.

Jen and I needed PBS to love us without reservation. But we passionately disagreed with their note about Peg's freaking out. So we explained our thoughts in a carefully-worded letter that was assertive and firm but respectful. And they said fine. They still loved us, enough to move us on to the final round of the competition in which we were commissioned to make a fully animated episode of *Peg + Cat*.

LESSON: Exclamation points can be good!

I've always resented the way kids TV writers are obliged to use exclamation points in scripts to reassure executives that the drama is dramatic. In scripts for the stage you're supposed to build the intensity into the lines themselves and let the actors decide where to place emphasis, so I wouldn't use an exclamation point in a play even if the character's line is "I realize I'm shouting but you're about to wipe out the entire human race." But working with Jen, exclamation points felt natural. She's sincerely upbeat, and has an anything-is-possible spirit that's truly beautiful. The exclamation points in her emails were genuine reminders that she was glad to be in touch with me. In response to her upbeat exclamations I exclaimed right back! And exclaimed in scripts! And we sure punctuated loudly when PBS reviewed our pilot and informed us that *Peg + Cat* was going to be a show!!!

Jen and I formed 100 Chickens Productions (originally called 9ate7 Productions until a company called 7ate9 Productions threatened to eat us) and found an office in Brooklyn where we'd oversee the making of *Peg + Cat*. As co-executive producers we shared all responsibilities, but Jen would take the lead on anything involving animation or design and I'd be in charge of the writing of 80 scripts.

After spending months creating the pilot script, I'd be responsible for 79 more scripts over the next couple years. The script for an 11-minute episode is 20 pages within which there has to be a story that teaches two math concepts to kids of various abilities while being constantly surprising and funny and there's lots of lyric writing along the way. A search for writers yielded only 3 that Jen and I felt could do all those things, but each of the 3 was in demand, and whether they had time for us or not I'd be responsible for making sure PBS had scripts that Jen and I loved and PBS loved in batches of four every six weeks.

When I sit down to write, something needs to happen that's out of my control. No matter how short the script or how many I've written, some fresh impulse needs to take me by surprise and carry me along or the script will suck. When working on a show I like, that always seems to happen. But I can't know that it will happen. I can't force it to happen...even when there's a massive production schedule spread across the wall of our conference room that says it has to happen.

While reading one of my first *Peg + Cat* scripts to Jen I found myself breathing in little gasps, it felt like my lungs were shaking. As my angst grew over the next couple months I consumed increasing quantities of Ativan and Klonopin until I'd wake up in the middle of the night with no idea whether the buzzing running through my limbs was caused by anxiety about 80 scripts or addiction to pills. On a family vacation at the New Jersey shore I became fixated on the idea that I was going to ruin the show. Jen's big break, the jobs of everyone in our company, this whole millions-of-dollars production was going to come crashing down because of me. I couldn't live with that feeling.

There was no way I was going to quit *Peg + Cat*, so I consulted a psychiatrist who had particular experience working with TV writers about finally going on an SSRI. After a week on the anti-anxiety SSRI Zoloft I was yawning a lot, my mouth felt dry, my orgasms were weak, and my anxiety was still getting worse.

LESSON: SSRIs can take a month to work.

After two and a half weeks on Zoloft I was in a cab rushing to a meeting, suddenly traffic came to a stop, we were stuck, I'd be late, I felt a mild pressure in my chest – and felt so happy. I'd been feeling a sharp pressure in my chest in tense situations for a month. (My heart was fine, I had that checked.) This mild pressure was a gentle tap compared to that. The next morning I woke up and all anxiety was gone.

LESSON: SSRIs can give you your life back.

Though I'd feared an SSRI would take over my brain the opposite was true, it set me free. Free of that constant dread, walking through the world felt so much easier. I wasn't scared of deadlines or meetings or responsibility or awkward conversations in the bathroom and couldn't wait to get to work every morning to attack those 80 scripts.

LESSON: You can use old structures to create new work.

In drama school I hated formal story structures and the theater of the past that bowed down to them. But while creating copious stories for *Peg + Cat* I found myself worshipping at the altar of the most common structure of them all, the Three Act Structure:

Act 1: It's a special day. Something happens to create a really big problem.

Act 2: The hero tries to solve the problem until something happens that forces the action to a climax in--

Act 3. The final show down. The problem is resolved.

As I worked with this structure I began to see it in the greatest of dramas --

Act 1: Something is rotten in the state of Denmark. The Ghost tells Hamlet to kill the King.

Act 2: As Hamlet plots against the King, the King sends Hamlet away on a ship but pirates send Hamlet back to Denmark where--

Act 3: Hamlet walks into the King's trap, and kills the King. And in the greatest of cartoons--

Act 1: A pretentious opera singer is annoying Bugs Bunny. The singer smashes Bugs' banjo -- This means war.

Act 2: Bugs pranks the opera singer but the singer keeps performing, until his opera enters its final act and--

Act 3: Bugs dresses up as Leopold Stokowski, has the opera singer hold a high note until his head turns red and his clothes fly off and the entire theater falls down.

A story can follow this (or any) format and still be stupid and boring. But by conceiving Peg's adventures in terms of the 3 act structure, I could be sure that no matter how much the script changed as composers, animators, and voice actors made their contributions, steps leading to a satisfying ending complete with a solved problem were in there somewhere. And though I used to associate structure with restriction, I found the opposite to be true; the structure was like a simple, steady chord progression over which our writers could jam with abandon.

Since Peg and Cat can go anywhere, stories could be set on a farm, at a circus, in a fairy tale kingdom...After a few episodes our heroes were helping Romeo reach Juliet's window using parallel lines. Story material was snatched from myths, nursery rhymes, legends, operas, and chicken jokes; we placed episodes in New Orleans, Mexico City, or 19th century Vienna because of the music associated with those locales, while the Wild West, medieval Japan, and outer space were chosen for the visuals. Jen and I loved going beyond the standard math curriculum to show the role creativity and imagination can play in solving problems, and to expose kids to ideas they could taste now and digest later, like the concept of infinity. In the name of girl power we gave Peg strong women pals like Queen Cleopatra, Billie Holliday, Marie Curie, Emily Dickinson, Peg's hippy Grandmom who's all about the 60s, and a female president of the United States voiced by Sandra Oh. We balanced the females with traditional boy stuff, like cool dudes, racecars, ball games, space ships, monsters, warriors, and gross sounds. (For the record, testing showed that boy viewers enjoyed the powerful females and the girls enjoyed the boy stuff, even the gross sounds.) And in keeping with the show's theme that math is for everyone, both Jen, who is of color, and her rosacean Caucasian collaborator took special pride in creating characters of different races, religions, backgrounds, and lifestyles; one of the best things about working for PBS is that you have the opportunity and obligation to reach the vast American Public.

While making our show, I realized that I have certain Rules for Making a Kids TV Show That Doesn't Suck:

1. Kid-friendly doesn't mean sterile. Anywhere there are humans there will be rivalries and crushes, whether they're the focus of the story or not.

2. Underwear, toilets, and body functions aren't offensive. Exposing kids to bland characters, trite morals, crappy designs, and cheesy songs is offensive.

3. Educational content should flow naturally through the drama. Don't stop the action for education.

4. Don't make a show 3-5 year olds can digest instantly that leaves everyone over the age of 5 bored out of their skull. Make a show that fascinates and mystifies kids that they can come back to and understand in new ways as they grow.

5. Keeping older kids and adults in the room with young viewers encourages shared laughter and discussion; it's better for everybody.

6. Don't try to appeal to adults by making wise-assed jokes that go over kids' heads. Appeal to adults by focusing on aspects of the world that are amazing.

7. If you care about kids: Don't read studies about them and make something they should like. Be a kid and make something you love.

8. As much singing and dancing around as possible, on screen and in life.

Jen felt like I did about all of the above. And as we put our iconoclastic principals into practice, I came to discover that:

LESSON: While working in television it's possible to express a pure, personal vision.

In other words:

LESSON: Entertainment can be art.

Art begins inside -- what you want to do. Entertainment begins outside -- what the public wants you to do. But while developing a work of art you should keep your audience in mind. And while working on an assignment driven by public tastes and needs, you should aim to please using your own personal vision and style. So jugglers can be artists. So can people who create commercial jingles. And as we found ways to teach math through character and story, I came to feel that:

LESSON: Education can be art.

In a way, every work of art is educational. Artists show the audience a certain piece of our world and point out surprising things about life. And the best educators link fact with feeling, wit, personality, and rhythm, conveying information with a sense of why you should care. The cool teacher is an artist. So is the imaginative biographer.

LESSON: When reinventing yourself remember: there are plenty of fields beyond those commonly considered arts that allow you to put your inner self out there.

While staying true to our own values Jen and I were able to avoid offending others, with a few exceptions...

*When a funder found our brash Toad character to be a Jewish stereotype we made the character more polite and less like every one of my uncles at Seder dinner.

*Poop is the sex of kids TV: the target audience loves it, but it has to be handled with care. Though PBS asked us to devote an entire episode to the art of pooping on the toilet, in other episodes they censored toilet talk, even the sound of an off camera flush, to avoid upsetting parents.

*When Jen conceived a 2D super villain named Flat Woman, I was concerned that the character's flat chest might call attention to a sensitive subject. But when Jen gave Flat Woman triangular boobs PBS found the character too "sadomasochistic", so Jen removed the chest triangles and everyone was fine with our flat Flat Woman.

*We were allowed to have our 3 Teen characters say "OMG" constantly because we insisted the G was for Goodness. But when the show began to air, some religious viewers told us what the G means to them -- which meant a lot of rewriting and redubbing for us.

Shortly after a script was written I'd notice on computer screens near mine: designs of sets and props from the episode, sketches of scenes being blocked out, a brand new character leaping and spinning for the first time. Beyond the desks with artists and animators was a cluster of desks where producers coordinated budgets and schedules with our animation partners in Toronto and financial partners in Pittsburgh while staying constantly in touch with our PBS friends in DC. At designated times a producer or two would lead Jen and me to the conference room to view an early pass of the story board (a series of sketches blocking out the action), or down the hall to the sound studio to hear a rough version of the music, or to direct voice actors, or view a fully animated episode. In giving notes my focus was always on clarity, making sure the words were audible and that what we were seeing supported what we were hearing. I especially loved being surprised by the work, as the show became an expression of the imagination and talent of everybody involved.

After we'd turned in many of those 80 episodes they began to air.

LESSON: The best thing about TV compared to theater: it's so public.

Every day people across the country saw our show. (PBS Kids viewership is measured in millions.)

LESSON: The worst thing about TV compared to theater: it's so private.

Everybody watches in small groups or alone; the authors can't be with their audience.

Though Jen and I didn't get to hear laughs and applause from our TV audience, we did get letters from parents and teachers, drawings from kids, clips of kids singing the songs, and Internet posts of all kinds. Sometimes I'd see images from our show on the TV screen in a restaurant, or hear a kid walking down the block singing our "Problem Solved" song. People who test educational shows to make sure kids are learning gave us high marks, groups that give seals of approval gave us seals of approval, and a group of our TV industry peers nominated *Peg + Cat* for Daytime Emmy Awards.

LESSON: If you don't get nominated for awards: Tell yourself they're subjective, arbitrary, and divisive, and you're lucky to save the time and money it takes to fly across the country for that pompous pointless overblown ceremony.

LESSON: If you do get nominated: Strut your stuff you big fat star.

Jen and I and a bunch of our Peg-mates got all dressed up and flew to LA and when the nominees for the Emmy for Best Animated Pre-K show were announced by a Muppet time stopped. "And the winner is..." said the Muppet, " *Peg + Cat.*" We jumped around and charged up to the stage and thanked everybody we knew and jumped around some more and as we exited the stage I kissed the Muppet on the lips. Shortly after we got home PBS hired us to make 50 more episodes of *Peg + Cat.*

While making that last big batch of shows, Jen and I went further in all directions, exploring ideas and images we'd carried around our whole lives. Some afternoons I'd break from writing to sample a double peanut butter blossom cookie baked by one of our designers or a piece of Butterfinger baklava baked by our story board guy and look out at those 2 dozen people working away at their computers and feel as happy as Beavis.

LESSON: Having a job can be cool.

※ ※ ※

CHAPTER 12:
LEARNING TO SAVE YOUR BRAIN

Shortly after *Peg + Cat* was nominated for a third batch of Emmys Jen and I observed a test PBS was doing of our show in DC, where the tester greeted us with her conclusion that we should make the show more "redundant" and "dumb it down". As we observed through a one-way window it seemed to me the tester was shushing the kids who enjoyed the show and coaxing others to say they couldn't follow the stories and didn't like the characters and didn't get the math. I wanted to scream every hateful word I knew at the tester and the PBS people who hired her but instead became so silent Jen worried about me.

A few days later in LA our show won its second Emmy Award for writing but when we got back to the office I looked at my screen and found that I couldn't write. I did pushups to calm myself down, then took Jen aside to explain that I couldn't write any more. She said it was okay, we'd completed the bulk of the writing, I could skip meetings and come in less often. At home I spent my time lying on the couch. It wasn't that I was sad, exactly. It was that nothing seemed worth doing. All meaning was gone from the world.

Lisa had learned to be patient with my moods but when I told her she should go to Anna's college graduation without me she knew something was way off. Our youngest was graduating from my own alma mater, she'd been elected to give a speech to the whole graduating class, but I didn't want to get up off the couch and get dressed.

In the days before my appointment with my psychiatrist I found myself sleeping for shorter and shorter intervals at night until I couldn't tell my conscious thought from dreams. As severed heads and squiggly dark shapes floated before my eyes I felt like I was hallucinating and feared I was becoming schizophrenic like my brother. When Lisa told me she loved me I asked why. I'd lost all interest in being alive. I knew the kids would grow up fine so what was I waiting around to see?

A recent *Scientific American* study confirms what fans of Van Gogh, Sylvia Plath, Virginia Woolf, or Kurt Cobain already know: the emotional sensitivity and constant questioning that allows artists to create corresponds with susceptibility to depression. People who make a life in the arts are 10 times more likely than everyone else to suffer from that dark disease. While the depression I'd had in drama school was a response to a tough situation, this was different; everything was going great and yet I was feeling a downward pull more powerful than anything I'd experienced.

When I got to see the psychiatrist he said my anger at the *Peg + Cat* tester could have been a trigger for my depression, as could a recent visit to my brother in which he didn't want to see me, but our talk about causes was brief, we got right to focusing on treatment. He put me back on Zoloft – I'd gotten off after an anxiety-free year – and put me on a regular dose of Ativan to make life bearable until the Zoloft kicked in. To help me sleep he also prescribed Trazodone, a mild anti-depressant that causes drowsiness.

The drugs allowed me to sleep 5-6 hours a night but waking up in the morning was horrible: The two things I absolutely could not do were 1) get up, 2) lie there. Eventually I'd bring myself downstairs, take my daily pills, then lie on the couch feeling the infinite moments of the day ahead pressing down on my chest. I had no idea how to get from one moment to the next, every second felt impossible to fill. I didn't want to listen to my CDs. Why make a piece of metal spin around above a beam of light. Why make my feet go in circles on the pedals of a bicycle. Why open a book and look at the words. At 11:00 AM and 3:00 PM I'd force myself to check my work email, make any script changes slowly, breathing deeply. The best part of the day was the end; in bed at night Lisa and I would hold onto one another and list specific things that were great about our kids until I fell asleep.

After a month the Zoloft hadn't done anything, which was disappointing and weird since it had worked so well before, so my psychiatrist had me raise the dosage. I went back to work, told everybody about my sickness, worked slowly and took lots of breaks. Jen coaxed me along in meetings, carried more than her share of the decision making, pointed out the positive as I saw only looming disaster. A month later still no improvement so we raised the dose again. At the higher dose I couldn't have an orgasm plus food began to taste awful, everything was too salty or too sweet. I'd lost my desire to eat anyway, had been forcing myself to drink protein shakes but was still losing weight fast. I couldn't even cry, the medicine didn't allow it, so there was no release of any kind.

As I feared I'd never get better life became like a continuous panic attack. Friends would tell me I was going to be okay and I believed them but if you're in an elevator that's gone into free fall you can say to yourself I know that cable thing will stop the fall in a moment but there's still that crisis feeling of adrenaline rushing all through you as the elevator just keeps falling. As the summer dragged on my hands were shaking so much I couldn't take a shirt off the hanger. I didn't dare try to eat food in front of people because they'd see my hands shaking as I attempted to get the fork to my mouth. Every morning I woke up and checked my hands but they were still shaking. When I met with my psychiatrist he was required to ask if I found life no longer worth living. I answered that I had no interest in killing myself but wished I could stop being alive until I was better. How did I get here? I asked myself over and over. The world outside my head had become unfathomable, but on the inside everything was out of control. I had no place to be.

While reading a book about depression that said some people are untreatable, I realized medicine might never help me, decided to take a cue from the Bible and act like a happy person until I became one. As my depression told me to stay in, don't get up, don't move, I did the opposite. My therapist told me to take in the world the way a dog does, noticing the sunshine on the leaves, the sound of water in a puddle, so I forced myself to walk outside every morning, noticing the sun, the leaves, and doing my best to smile. It was fake. I knew that. But I kept pretending. I went to yoga, took basic classes, stayed in the back of the class so no one would notice my legs shaking, resented the teacher every time she told us to move from one position to another but did everything she said and kept coming back for more. One day I wound up in a more demanding yoga class where instructor Miriam Wolf had us reach our arms out to the sides and swirl them in circles for minutes as a driving pop song played until everyone was groaning but Miriam cheered us on over the music: "It hurts because you're growing. It hurts because you're getting stronger." We groaned louder and shouted and kept going.

LESSON: Growth is struggle.

LESSON: Everybody's fighting to get through the day.

LESSON: It's hard work having a brain.

LESSON: My brother works with his brain to get through the day. So does everyone.

LESSON: It's a fight to express yourself and a fight to be heard.

LESSON: It's a fight to find meaning in your life and a fight to keep it there.

LESSON: Even when you don't want to keep dancing you can keep dancing.

LESSON: Keep dancing.

LESSON: Keep dancing.

LESSON: Keep dancing.

After my summer in hell with no improvement my psychiatrist asked if I wanted to raise the Zoloft a third time, I said please no more of those Zoloft side effects so he put me on a beginning dosage of Prozac which is also known for treating depression and had worked with a couple members of my family (there's definitely a genetic component to depression). Soon pizza tasted good again. Was my hand trembling less? Was the smile with which I greeted the trees and puddles finally real? When I asked Lisa if Prozac had made me better she said no, I didn't have my zip back – that was her measure. And Lisa was right, there was still no lightness in my mood, no joy. My therapist agreed with Lisa, said I shouldn't have to work so hard to fill up my time and make an effort to convince myself I'm happy, I should be able to just sit there and look out the window and feel good. What a far-away dream that felt like, the days when I could sit there and feel good.

LESSON: Keep trying things.

My therapist and psychiatrist were frequently in touch about me, both kept reminding me never to give up, if something doesn't work try something else, and they always had more ideas. In October my psychiatrist switched me from Prozac to Effexor, a drug that's similar to an SSRI but particularly effective with obsessive-compulsive symptoms. After a couple weeks on Effexor the shaking in my hands lessened. I would hear music and find myself moving to it. I would see a donut and want to eat it. I found myself yapping out bad puns and annoying non sequiturs with Lisa. My zip! When people wanted to take a group picture

I would put my arm around the people on either side of me and smile. When a friend asked if I wanted to get together I would say yes and mean it. I enjoyed talking with friends. And strangers. Just walking down the block I would say hello to everyone who was willing to make eye contact. When it was rainy or cloudy or cold I didn't feel a vague fear and sadness I just opened an umbrella or put on a coat. As the sun set earlier each day it didn't mean darkness and old age it meant the beginning of fall which is a lovely season. In the office I could sit beside Jennifer Oxley and feel like challenges had a softness around the edges, all hurtles would be cleared, missions would be accomplished, everything would somehow work out. I had emerged from six months of depression.

LESSON: Depression ends.

The fall of 2016 was a strange time to be happy in Brooklyn, as the election of not America's first woman president but Donald Trump had everybody walking around stunned and/or sobbing. Though I had to repress my post depression urge to break into song every time I entered a room, I was able to make use of my revived spirit to support shaken friends, family, co-workers, and yogis, soothing them with nostalgic tales of how when Ronald Reagan became president we were sure he was going to start a nuclear war (He totally didn't!).

LESSON: On the other side of depression: elation.

Sunny to the point of being annoying, I had come to believe -- and still do -- that if you can get over your fear of falling down and keep getting back up:

LESSON: Anyone can do anything.

The premiere of the *Peg + Cat* episode "The Eid Al Adha Aventure" that fall turned out to be timely, since Trump's depiction of Muslims as clannish anti-Americans was encouraging open hostility towards American Muslims. Like our Christmas and Hanukkah episodes, the Eid episode features math, traditional music and culture, and a story that celebrates the spirit of the holiday: Peg's pal Jasmine wears a hijab and her brother Amir rocks out on the oud as they sing the Arabic holiday greeting "Eid Mubarek" with Peg and Cat. Since the holiday is about giving to those with less (less = math) the kids and Cat bring honey cake to Peg's grownup pal Mac who can't make it to the soup kitchen because he stubbed both of his big toes.

When "The Eid Al Adha Adventure" aired we got more mail than ever, all of it positive, all of it emotional. Parents described their kids crying for joy to see their family's holiday celebrated by their TV friends Peg and Cat. One Mom wrote that she'd been afraid to send her kid to kindergarten because of how Muslims were being looked at with suspicion, another wrote that the day before her teacher had said her child had an "unpronounceable name", but the broadcast of our Eid episode on national TV made these parents and many more feel hopeful and welcome in America. Parents of other faiths wrote in too, grateful that their kids were learning about their classmates and neighbors with backgrounds different from their own. Since roughly one percent of Americans are Muslim, a profit-driven network would be unlikely to make an Eid Al Adha special. Only PBS is dedicated solely to serving the people and making America better.

LESSON: I heart PBS.

And, harder for me to admit:

LESSON: TV and other forms of electronic mass media can do good.

As in a fairy tale, the last song in the last episode of *Peg + Cat*, "Making a World with my Friend", won the show's last Emmy. With *Peg* winding down Jen and I were invited to create new kids shows for PBS, Disney, Nickelodeon, and everybody else. We pitched ideas, were hired to develop them for weeks/months/years, but nothing turned into our next big original show so we let our dream team go, Jen formed her own company, and I returned to civilian life feeling so great about the time I'd spent with Jennifer Oxley. For the greater part of a decade she and I

had worked side by side, jumping around and singing the *Peg +
Cat* theme song (I played uke) at toy fairs or book stores, trav-
eling across the country and overseas for work-related adventures, and sitting at adjacent desks in our beloved Brooklyn
office. Even after a long day of recording sessions and conference calls the two of us would sometimes take the subway home
together and get into such focused conversation about the show
that we'd miss our stop. But the best part of our relationship lived
in silence. Jen and I just got each other. She made me feel supported and trusted so completely that in her company I could be
prolific, silly and serious in a whole new way.

LESSON: It's worth the wait for the right collaborator.

※ ※ ※

CHAPTER 13:

LIVING ON WHEN YOU'RE GONE

A few months before this book was published something happened that changed my perspective on everything I'd written so far.

The story begins in the spring of 2021 when I got an email from the dramaturg at Sweden's Malmö Opera asking about *Flurry Tale*, a Christmas opera she'd read about on my website. **LESSON: Have a website.**

Composer Rusty Magee and I created *Flurry Tale* in 1994 and developed it with guidance from American Opera Projects in a series of workshops and performances in churches and schools until 2000. Rusty and I adored the piece, revised and edited constantly, hoped that one of those presentations would lead to production. But as the years went by and nobody stepped up to produce *Flurry Tale* I convinced myself the show was too scary for kids and too silly for adults. **LESSON: You're not bad. The world is slow.**

After reviewing the score and libretto, the folks at Malmö decided to produce *Flurry Tale* in the winter of 2023. I could hardly process the news. Our opera would have a grand world premiere on one of Europe's largest stages nearly 30 years after it was created, and 20 years after Rusty Magee died of cancer.

At the first virtual production meeting I offered the director and producer some cuts to keep the show moving swiftly. They listened politely but weren't interested in cutting. In fact, they wanted to use every note in the score, even the overture and a song we would always omit. They also planned to have Santa's toys come to life to form a chorus of dancers, doubling the size of our 6-character cast. While prior performances of *Flurry Tale* had been accompanied by solo piano, the music was now being scored for Malmö's 47-piece orchestra. The libretto was being translated into Swedish so it could engage newcomers to opera who don't speak English; the title would be *Vinteryra*, pronounced "vin ter OOO ruh," which means winter madness.

My trip to Sweden for the opening involved taking three different planes over the course of a single timeless evening. But the walk from my hotel to the Malmö Opera House was only ten minutes, about as long as the first walk I took from my Hell's Kitchen apartment to the Met. The screen above the theater showed a colorful graphic announcing: *"Turandot."* After a few seconds it shifted to: *"Don Giovanni."* And then: *"Vinteryra."*

As the overture began, the sweeping chords played on a full string section cut right into me, made me so happy. Twenty seconds later the trombones and tympani captured a boisterous romping vibe that made me laugh. I missed Rusty. While creating the opera during those snowy New York winters of the 90s, Rusty and I were raising young kids and trying to piece together an income. He had worked so hard to get every note right, but he never got to hear his score played by a full orchestra. The moment was tragic, but it was wonderful too. Five hundred people were paying attention. My friend was gone but not forgotten.

LESSON: Your work can be appreciated when you're gone.

In fact...

LESSON: It's quite common that when a work of art is being appreciated, the creator is long gone.

As the performance continued it seemed that Malmö exists in a parallel universe where everything's bigger and better. The Sugar Plum Fairy entered flying twenty feet above the stage, toys rose up from below and grew to human-size, the Snow Man character emerged from a giant snow sculpture that opened and closed, Santa and his Reindeer rode in on a full-sized sleigh. The revolving stage, the set pieces flying up and down, the trippy lighting and wild costumes...every element of this production intensified the bizarre delight we were going for.

LESSON: Minimal can be cool. So can maximal.

Rusty was all over the place on that stage; his wit, heart, love of rocking out. I was there too. As the little girl character Emma struggles to get her Dad to understand things he can't see, I remembered how my own little girl and boy could see things that were invisible to me. The inner workings of young-parent me were being exposed by these performers with fresh vigor.

My favorite music in the show is the quartet about forgiveness near the end. Originally we had the four characters sing the same lyrics in four-part harmony. When the music director of American Opera Projects suggested we have them sing four different lines at the same time, Rusty burst into tears. It was going to be so much work to figure out all those new melodies and harmonies, we'd been working on the show for years, it never seemed to be done...But Rusty knew the change would be best for the opera, so he came up with four completely different parts. And now his expression of glorious forgiveness was calling out to people in a faraway land, many of whom hadn't been born when he wrote the notes.

At the end of the performance a boy sitting next to me cheered loudly. I told him I wrote the words. He gave me a high-five. Then I rushed backstage and hugged the performers and director, choreographer, conductor...Those were some of my favorite hugs ever, and I've had some great hugs.

LESSON: Even your most neglected work can find its perfect home in time.

As I write this I'm 67 years old. Though I still wonder whether the thing I'm writing will ever find its audience, remembering Malmö helps me live with that uncertainty. Art has a relationship to the universe that I can't begin to understand. So I'm trying to relax and enjoy the ride.

LESSON: Imagine your Malmö.

Believe in it.

※ ※ ※

POSTSCRIPT

When I was 6, while playing with the collection of sparkly rocks I kept in the basement, I made up a song "Beautiful is This and That" and imagined that my song would become everyone's song, people everywhere would see the incredible coolness that I was starting to see all over the place and share my excitement and we'd all hold hands and sing together. As I pursued my career in the arts I came to see how hard it is to get everyone — or anyone — to see what you're seeing and feel what you're feeling. Each of us is alone in our own head experiencing the world our own way, working to develop powerful intimate connections with a few other people over the course of a lifetime.

But while I was writing this book it came back, that hopeful feeling from childhood, whenever I feel good about what I'm writing it comes back and gives me a push to keep going. And even though I know my work won't magically transform the world, I know it won't bring people together in harmony like musical notes, I still *feel* that it will, that I'll be walking around and I'll sense that everything is a little different, we'll all be regarding each other in a different way, we'll understand something, all of us, at the same time, and share a feeling of dancing and discovery and flying and music, and no one will feel alone.

THE END

THANKS

To my agent Maryann Karinch and publisher Ben Ohmart: Thank you.

To Cristina Tarantola for the cover photo and Robbie Adkins for the book design: Thank you.

For helping with the manuscript, to Dare Clubb, Constance Hale, Christine Hemp, Gail Hochman, Jonathan Raab, Jordan Rodman, and Alexandra Shelley: Thank you.

To the girls who broke my heart, thanks for driving me to the theater.

To my mom Joanne Morgan, thanks for driving me to the theater and picking me up afterwards.

Thanks to my dad Willard Aronson.

Thanks to my sister Dorothy.

Thanks to my brother Joe.

Thanks to Lisa Vogel for help with the editing, Jake Aronson for help with my branding, and Anna Aronson for helping me to be less offensive.

In the text I avoided shouting out to friends/family/coworkers whenever possible even when they were a big part of the story, but at this point I'm going to shout out thanks to Josh Nadel, Richard Smith, Eric Weiner, Alan MacVey, Larry Vogel, Daniel Berkowitz, Judith Aronson, Lori Stephens, Noah Aronson, Frank Morgan, Rob Suher, Wayne Ury, Carol Nadell, Jose Colon, Stacey Greenberger, Billy Lopez, Chris Jammal, Erica Kepler, Rhonda Roumani, Asra Husain, Tim Cornell, Amy Aquino, Angela Kmeck, Ann Klotz, Daniel Greenberg, Anna Cascio, Erik Ehn, Leah Greene, Curt Dempster, William Carden, Sonya Sobieski, Robert Davenport, Ellen Mareneck, Chris Smith, June Blotnick, Jurgen Kern, Jane Abernethy, Duncan Brine, Angel Garcia, Bob Tushman, Ellen Moskowitz, Natalie Engel, Linda Simensky, Kim Berglund, Christopher Gould, Marie Parker Shaw, Jihye Lee, and every one of my yoga teachers.